Mansi: A Rare Man in His Own Way

TAYEB SALIH

Mansi: A Rare Man in His Own Way

Translated from the Arabic
by Adil Babikir

Banipal Books

Mansi: A Rare Man in His Own Way
First published in English translation
by Banipal Books, London 2020

This translation © The Estate of Tayeb Salih, 2019

First published in Arabic 2004
Original title: منسي: إنسان نادر على طريقته
Mansi: Insaan Nadir ala Tariqatihi
published by Riad El Rayyes, Beirut 2004.
© The Estate of Tayeb Salih 2009

A CIP record for this book is available in the British Library
ISBN 978-0-9956369-8-9
E-book: ISBN: 978-0-9956369-9-6

Banipal Books
1 Gough Square, LONDON EC4A 3DE, UK
www.banipal.co.uk/banipalbooks/

Banipal Books is an imprint of Banipal Publishing
Typeset in Bembo

Mansi and Tayeb Salih

Tayeb Salih:
Non-Fiction Writing at its Best

With only three novels, written between 1966 and 1976, Tayeb Salih rose to international fame as one of the greatest novelists of our time.

His *Season of Migration to the North* has been making waves throughout the Arab world since it was first published in 1966, and across the globe once it appeared in Denys Johnson-Davies's English translation in 1969. The highly celebrated novel immediately received critical acclaim as "among the finest six novels to be written in modern Arabic literature" in the words of Edward Said, and the most important Arabic novel of the 20th century, according to the Damascus-based Arab Literary Academy. It has been translated into more than 20 languages and selected by the Norwegian Book Club among the world's top 100 works of all time.

While Salih has continued to be in the spotlight among critics and academia, with scores of critiques and scholarly articles focused on his work, he remained virtually unproductive for almost a decade. His last novel, *Bandarshah*, was published in two parts in 1971 and 1976.

However, starting from the late 1980s, Salih appeared every week on the last page of the London-based *Al-Majalla* magazine and over the next ten years captivated readers with his fine writings on diverse topics, including literary criticism, political commentary and reflections on life. These writings were later published in a collection of ten volumes.

One of the ten was the book in question here, published for the first time in English translation – *Mansi: A Rare Man in His Own Way*. The Arabic *Mansi: Insaan Nadir ala Tariqatihi* had been published in weekly instalments, starting in 1988, before being collected together and published in 2004. It is a unique type of writing, combining biography, autobiography, political analysis, and philosophical insight with a great sense of humour and satire.

Salih points out from the outset that the person he is writing about is not someone of note. "Yet, he was important in the eyes of a few, including myself, who accepted him as he was and loved him regardless. He was a man who had traversed life's short journey in leaps and bounds, occupied more space than had been allocated for him, and caused quite a clamour within the realm of his existence."

With that introduction, Salih sets us off on a hilarious journey with a friend whose rashness and indifference cause Salih tremendous embarrassment and almost costs him his job. Yet, the way Salih portrays Mansi strongly suggests the profound love he held for him.

Although Salih repeatedly pointed out that all the events in this book were "factual anecdotes", many in the Arab world have misread the book as a novel. The confusion is partly related to Mansi, who has a unique blend of traits typical of a fictional character. A man who lived with at least three different names, and who played at least eight real time roles, from a porter to a university lecturer, and from a nurse to a clown. A penniless man who rose to the upper echelons of British society and married a girl from a prominent English family, a descendant of Sir Thomas More. A man daring enough to cross all security and protocol barriers – presenting himself to Queen Elizabeth as the head of an official Egyptian delegation, and engaging in a public debate, on a subject he knew little about, with no less a historian than Arnold Toynbee.

But it also had to do with Salih's writing style. In *Mansi*, and invariably in all his other non-fiction writing, including even political commentary, Salih skilfully employs fiction-writing techniques to weave texts that seem to slip through the borders of genres. His amazing ability to mould his ideas into a captivating, coherent, and well-knitted narrative is evident throughout this book.

Another unique advantage of this book is that it provides

a rare exposure to Salih's personal life as it contains glimpses of his career years at the BBC, at UNESCO, and of his social encounters with friends in Cairo, Beirut, and other cities. Here, Salih comes out into the open without the usual camouflage of the fiction writer, unlike in his novels where he consistently hides behind an unnamed narrator who has some aspects in common with him. Through the lens of this exposure, we see a highly satirical Salih with a keen sense of humour. We also see a collected person who remains unflappable in the face of the most delicate challenges.

Apart from *Mansi*, the ten-volume collection, published by the Beirut-based Riad El-Rayyes publishing house and the Omdurman-based Abdel Karim Mirghani Center, included a volume on al-Mutanabbi, which contains thought-provoking insights into the verse of this legendary poet for whom Salih showed great admiration, calling him "the master".

Another volume, dubbed *Fi Rehab al-Janadriyah and Asilah* (About al-Janadriyah and Asilah), focuses on two prominent cultural festivals hosted by Saudi Arabia and Morocco respectively. A third, *Al-Mudi'oun kal-Nujoom* (Prominent Stars), discusses the works and ideas of some prominent figures from the East and West.

The list from the West includes British politician Rab Butler (Lord Butler), British journalist Michael Adams, French literary critic and theorist Roland Barthes, British historian and journalist A. J. P. Taylor, French novelist Marcel Proust, and others. There are also dedicated volumes about

Sudan, travel commentary, and other topics.

In his introduction to the ten-volume collection, Salih's lifetime friend, the late Mahmoud Salih, wrote: "To me, Tayeb Salih is an all-rounder, with a well-founded knowledge drawn from extensive readings across linguistics, religion, philosophy, politics, psychology, anthropology, literature, poetry, drama, and media, in both Arabic and English. This collection stands witness to his superb ability to captivate readers with great narratives, analysis, criticism, and insights."

There is consensus among those who read the original Arabic version of *Mansi* that only a few writers can write non-fiction as poetically and lyrically as Salih. Perhaps many of those who come to read this English translation will have the same impression.

Adil Babikir
January 2020

1

The man who died about this time last year [1987] was hardly anyone of consequence. Yet, he was important in the eyes of a few, including myself, who accepted him as he was and loved him regardless. He was a man who had traversed life's short journey in leaps and bounds, occupied more space than had been allocated for him, and caused quite a clamour within the realm of his existence.

He had assumed several names: Ahmed Mansi Yousif, Mansi Yousif Bastawrous and Michael Joseph; and had played several different roles: porter, nurse, teacher, actor, translator, writer, university lecturer, and clown. He was born to a faith different to the one he embraced along the way until his death, leaving behind Christian sons as well as a Muslim widow and sons. When I first met him, he was penniless. When he died, he left behind an estate of 200 acres of the best land in southern England, that included a huge and luxurious mansion with a swimming pool, stables and a fleet of cars: Rolls Royce, Cadillac, Mercedes, Jaguar, and other makes. He also left behind a 200-acre ranch in

Virginia, USA, as well as a restaurant and a travel agency.

When I heard the news of his death, I called his home in Tatchbury, on the outskirts of Southampton. A young voice answered, in an American accent. It was his eldest son, Simon, who told me his father had been in perfect health until a few weeks before when he developed a fatal liver tumour. I had been in the Sudan at the time. It occurred to me to ask about the funeral. He said a funeral had not yet been arranged, ten days after his death. They had been waiting for some formalities to be finalised before going ahead with the cremation. "But your father is Muslim," I told him, "and cremation is forbidden in Islam."

"We don't know about his conversion," he said. "What we do know is that our father was Christian and he used to tell us: 'Cremate my body when I die'."

"Look," I said, "your father was indeed a Muslim. There is no doubt about it – and I was witness to his conversion. It's a serious act to cremate the body of a Muslim. And remember, he left behind a Muslim widow and Muslim son, who is now your brother. Saying your father was not Muslim is equivalent to saying his marriage to that woman was illegal."

I called up his wife in Riyadh, who appealed to the Saudi Ministry of Foreign Affairs for help. And thanks to the latter's intervention, the matter was finally settled, and Mansi, as we used to call him, was given an Islamic burial ceremony a month or so after his death. However, *Al-Ahram* newspaper reported that his relatives in Egypt held a mass at a Coptic church. In my grief, I could not help but laugh.

2

That's truly what Mansi was, I said to myself, a living mystery in both his life and his death. He had always perplexed those around him when he was alive – and now, as a dead man, he was no less perplexing. To him, life was a big joke – an endless laugh, or as he put it, 'a series of crafty games'.

He was born into a Coptic family in the town of Mallawi, deep in Upper Egypt, where he grew up. Having spent most of his time with Muslim boys of his age, he was closer to Muslims than to Copts. Although the eldest son in the family, he was a young boy when his mother died. His father remarried and had other children. They were poor but proud. And it was with great difficulty that he made his way to university. He studied English at the University of Alexandria and I can think of only a few among my Arab acquaintances who were as proficient as he was in English. Yet, it was futile to put across to anyone that this chatty dilettante could excel in anything. I, for one, spent years trying to convince people that he was a truly gifted person.

His love for the English language naturally led him to England, where he landed in 1952, after a series of adventures and ploys. He got himself admitted to the University of Liverpool. Being penniless, he had to work to support himself, taking part-time jobs as a porter, a dishwasher and a nurse. Then he moved to London. In all his moves, as he later told us, he made approaches to philanthropic societies and churches, pulling as many strings as he could.

I met him in 1953, when I had just joined the BBC Arabic service. We would give him some script-writing or translation jobs, sometimes minor roles in our drama programmes to help him support himself through his studies. He had always had a strong passion for acting. Even after he became rich, he kept coming to us seeking to take part in our drama activities and would insist on being paid. And I used to tell him: "You're a good actor in life, but a lousy one on stage".

Before we became close friends, he once visited me at home – he lived in Fulham, not too far from my home in South Kensington. He presented me with a pair of socks of poor quality.

"What is this?" I asked.

"A present."

"What's the occasion?"

"Your birthday."

"What birthday? Today's not my birthday. Are you trying to bribe me?"

"Sort of," he said, laughing.

"You are hopeless. Even when you decide to bribe me, you choose something that's worth only two shillings?"

He showed no sign of being embarrassed, though. That was one of his unique attributes: he never felt shy, deterred, or embarrassed.

Letting out a childish laugh deep from his heart, he said: "Well, I thought I should give it a try. Who knows?"

After that we became close friends. Of all our mutual friends, I was to become like a godfather to him, although we were about the same age. That was perhaps because the others – Abdel Moneim El Rifaie, Akram Salih, Abdel Hai

Abdallah, Nadeem Sawalha and more – all treated him curtly and didn't take him seriously. Deep down, though, they all truly loved him.

2

Were Mansi an inch or two shorter, he would have been regarded as a pygmy. With age he became flabby, having a large pot belly and protruding bottom, which made him look more like a ball cut into two halves: upper and lower. He paid great attention to his appearance: he would wear silk shirts and fine suits that he bought at very low prices. At first he used to buy his suits from a tailor near Holborn, who bought the fabrics at wholesale prices from Dormeuil, the well-known shop in Piccadilly. One day, the tailor was too busy to go to Dormeuil, so Mansi offered to go in his place. Taking advantage of that opportunity, he registered his name as a tailor with Dormeuil and acquired a membership card that allowed him from then on to buy fabrics at wholesale prices. But, I have to admit, he was so generous with us that he would allow us to go with him to Dormeuil's and buy what we needed at his discounted rate.

Using his extraordinary skills, he discovered a smart tailor in the poorer East End of London, who charged a quarter of the rates of central London tailors. From that moment, this tailor became his permanent choice. Even after migrating to the United States, where he made a fortune, he continued to come back to London specifically to buy new suits and shirts. He would still buy the fabric from Dormeuil and deliver it to his favourite tailor in the East End. He would have dozens of suits and shirts made during a single visit, and he must have left behind a great number that unfortunately no one else could make use of, as I am sure there was not another person in the whole world who could fit into Mansi's suits.

Nonetheless, he never lacked the company of girls, who would fall in love with him. Some were remarkably beautiful, and tall. When he swaggered along beside one of them, he would look like a *doum* tree dwarfed by a palm tree. He had a radiant, almost round face and wide saucy eyes that he would fix on the speaker without blinking. Knowing that of him, we would tease him into breaking his constant gaze and he would succumb helplessly, bursting into a childish fit of laughter.

He was also witty and had an excellent command of the English language. He was bold enough to storm into any group of people, taking liberties with them as if he were a longtime acquaintance, giving the impression that the person he was talking to – however high-ranking they might be – was inferior to him. I took him to my convocation day where, for the first time, he met an Arab ambassador and his wife, both from a ruling family. I had to leave him briefly in their company and when I came back, I was stunned to see him standing between them and patting them on their shoulders, saying between persistent chuckles: "Ah, do keep talking. What cute accents you have!"

I drew him away. "Are you crazy?" I said. "Don't you know who they are?"

"And who on earth are they?" Even when I explained, he just said: "So what?"

Impudence was a help to him in some instances, but harmful in others. With women, however, in most cases it was a great help!

He told us once that in Liverpool he had fallen in love with a girl. They became engaged and a date was set for their wedding but unfortunately she died in a tragic car accident. He said she was his first and last love and that he would remain faithful to her memory forever and would never get married. Mansi had a strange way of expressing sadness: he would tell you he was sad, but you would not see any traces of it on him. We were taken by surprise when, shortly after that episode, he came to tell us he had got married. We then found out he had married a girl from a prominent English family, a descendant of Sir Thomas More. Some of us knew who Sir Thomas More was, but those who did not gave Mansi a golden opportunity to boast about it and explain everything to those of us who knew as well to those who did not, and in a scholarly English as if we were in a classroom:

"Sir Thomas More, the great-grandfather (many times over) of my beloved wife, is the minister and philosopher and author of *Utopia*. Of course you haven't heard of *Utopia*, Abdel Hai. What an ignoramus you are! He was senior minister to King Henry VIII. Yes, that same king famous for his six marriages. The King sentenced Sir Thomas More to death for refusing to pay allegiance to him when he separated the Church of England from the Vatican authority in Rome. Sir Thomas More also objected to the King's divorcing his wife Catherine of Aragon in order to marry Anne Boleyn. Understood, ignorant bunch? And oh yeah . . . remember Robert Bolt's play, *A Man for all Seasons*? That was about Sir Thomas More. He, in a nutshell, is the ancestor of my beloved wife."

In such situations, Mansi would be at his best, boasting about his impeccable English and in-depth knowledge of English history. Now, he seemed to have another reason for boasting: he had himself become a part of English history. Adding to our surprise, we understood that the bride, over and above all that history, was an up-and-coming pianist who played in concerts at the famous Wigmore Hall.

"But what on earth would make such a respectable lady fall in love with a mule like you?" Abdel Raheem asked.

He told us he had met her at a meeting of the Young Conservatives, the youth wing of the Conservative Party, where Mansi had a heated discussion with no less a figure than Sir Anthony Eden, Britain's Prime Minister at the time. I am going to tell you later how Mansi outsmarted one of Britain's most skilful politicians in a debate on the Palestinian cause, of which he knew little. But that night at the Young Conservatives Mansi believed he was great, dealing verbal blows at Eden, that veteran diplomat and politician. Mansi defended Egypt's decision to nationalise the Suez Canal and criticised the Eden government's adversarial policy towards Egypt. After the meeting, a kindhearted young woman approached Mansi to express her admiration of his courageous defence of his country. She invited him home and introduced him to her family. That very night, Mansi decided to marry her.

Thus Mansi underwent a complete transformation. From his small room in Fulham, he moved to a two-storey house on the famous Sydney Street in the posh district of Chelsea, where Mary and her mother lived on their own, her sister and two brothers having all married and moved elsewhere. In no time, Mansi became the undisputed master of that conservative English house. His mother-in-law, who had been brought up by French governesses and spoke English with a French accent, lived on the ground floor, so he took over the entire upper floor. Whenever we visited him, we would see him running around, up and down, issuing orders. He turned that house upside down and it would never have crossed the minds of Mary's noble ancestors, lying in peace in their graves in the English countryside, that the kind of people who now frequented their home would ever set a foot there. Call on Mansi at home, and once he opened the door, cooking smells of *molokheya, kammoneyah, kawarie,* and *masaqaa*[1] would invade your nostrils: smells that would have caused the intestines of those ancestors to writhe as they lay in their remote graveyards.

Abdel Hai, who was doing his PhD in economics at

---

1 Popular Egyptian dishes

Oxford, said, in his favourite accent of Egyptian Delta peasants: "How ironic, you *saeedi*[2], Coptic son of a . . . coming to England and ending up marrying a descendant of Sir Thomas More?"

Mansi's torso, now showing signs of indulgence and a comfortable life, shook with laughter, his round face grew taut and his saucy eyes radiated with that childish laughter which was part of his appeal: "You just don't understand, you poor peasant. Do you think it's a big deal? Who cares about Sir Thomas More? Don't forget I'm a descendant of the Pharaohs, the kings of Upper Egypt!"

"Who's a descendant of Pharaoh Kings? You're a descendant of the beggars of Upper Egypt!"

"Shut up, peasant! Just listen to what he's saying! And he's here to do a PhD in economics. What a joke! What have peasants got to do with economics?"

---

2 A person from Upper Egypt

3

Mansi was blessed with two wonderful qualities: genuine sympathy towards poor people, and faithfulness. He managed to maintain all the friendships he had developed over the years, adding many more along the way. He had an amazing ability to make, and maintain, acquaintances and friends of all races, sects, tastes and ranks. And he treated them all – the prince and the pauper alike – on equal terms, in his amazing down-to-earth way. He accorded special attention to poor people, and to children with whom he would be carefree and truly himself. With children, he was transformed into a child himself, and was very much one of them.

During his first visit to Doha – in the early 1970s, when I had just arrived there – he managed in a very short time to develop the acquaintance of a large number of people, who still remember him and ask about him, particularly taxi drivers.

He was the type of man who would leave a lasting impression on people – a good one in most cases, and a feeling of annoyance and alienation in rare instances. In all cases, however, whoever happened to meet him never forgot him.

No wonder, then, that he found old friends wherever he went. When he travelled with me to India and Australia, a trip I will tell you about later, a young man visited him in our hotel in Sydney. I noticed that he treated Mansi with profound respect. When I asked him why, Mansi said: "He's the son of X, the butcher in Sloane Street – remember him?"

The first time I went to that butcher's shop with Mansi, the butcher gave me a huge quantity of meat but charged me an incomparably small price. "There must be a miscalculation," I told him. "This meat should cost much more." Looking around the crowded shop, he finally said: "You're right. I'm sorry." He took the meat back, scaled it down to the quantity I had requested, and charged me a much higher price.

As we went out, Mansi said angrily: "When will you stop being such a dumb person? He was trying to give you special treatment because I'd told him you're a friend of mine."

"You should have told me," I said. "I thought it was a miscalculation on his part. How could I know you play your devious games even with butchers?"

But that particular incident was not one of his devious games, as I later came to understand. It was that butcher who had offered Mansi accommodation when he first arrived in London, treating him very much as a member of his own family. Mansi remained faithful to him for the rest of his life. When he became rich, one of his presents to his friend the butcher was a Rover car.

In Sydney, I asked Mansi why that young man had treated him with profound respect. "Because I saved him from what would have been a gloomy future. Had it not been for me, he wouldn't have gone to university and become an engineer."

His friend the butcher was a member of a strict religious sect that lived so apart from society that they would not even send their children to school. But Mansi kept after his friend until he convinced him to send his son, his eldest, to school.

"Were it not for me," Mansi boasted, "the fellow could have ended up a butcher in Smithfield Market or a porter in the Port of London."

"You should have gone a step further," I said, "and helped the man convert to Islam. You could have earned bountiful rewards."

Laughing at my comment, he said: "I surely would have done that if I myself had not been an infidel at the time. But, mind you, in America I have helped dozens convert to Islam."

"*Sobhan Allah*! Praise God!" I exclaimed. "What an irony! An infidel turned preacher!"

That remark sent him into a fit of giggles. Paradoxes of life always thrilled him and refreshed his soul in the same way water injected life into the stems of plants: "Just

---

3 Descendants of Prophet Mohammed.

imagine: someone like me marrying a lady from the *Ashraf*[3], while Muslims and sons of Muslims like you, get married to English ladies, or Swiss, and I don't know what!"

When we were in Sydney he was also visited by an Egyptian lady along with her Australian husband. He said he had known her and her family during his time as a student at Alexandria University. It had been thirty years since he had last seen her so they spent the evening reminiscing about their days in Alexandria. The lady was very happy, laughing as Mansi kept asking after every member of her family: what happened to X, and where had Y ended up now. "This is the Michael I have often spoken about," she said to her smiling husband. "He adored me and wanted to marry me. Right, Michael?"

I said to Mansi in Arabic: "You're back to Michael now? Didn't you convert to Islam and change your name to Ahmed?"

Another fit of his seemingly endless laughter syndrome followed. Being in Sydney was great fun and he was at his best; it mattered little, thirty years back, whether his name was Michael or Ahmed.

Nothing could have deterred him from inviting to lunch or dinner all the old friends he came across in Sydney – at my expense, though. He would sign the bill, charging it to my room number. That gave him a source of overwhelming joy, and he kept relating the story numerous times, each time with unfaltering excitement and the same lively heartfelt laugh. To him, there was nothing more amusing than proving how smart he was and how dumb I was.

No wonder then, that Mansi became a well-known figure in the whole of South West London, and beyond. He was famous in West Kensington, Earl's Court, South Kensington, Chelsea, Sloane Square, Belgravia, and Mayfair. He knew vegetable sellers, butchers, owners of restaurants, pubs and coffee shops, doctors and nurses in hospitals, police officers, shop workers, grocers, actors and actresses, MPs, university lecturers, clerics – people from all walks of life. They were by no means casual acquaintances. They were all true friends, exchanging visits at their homes. Mansi had tremendous energy, a Napoleonic energy as he called it. He had a car that was known as a bubble car because it looked like a soap bubble. True to its name, it made a brief appearance on the roads at the time before vanishing altogether.

Mansi used to ride around on a bike when he first came to London but after getting married and moving to Sydney Street, he bought that strange bubble car. I would occasionally go for a drive with him and you would see us in Piccadilly in the heaviest of traffic, wedged between two of London's red double-decker buses. The sight of that ugly car with its glass rooftop and the two of us squashed inside would stir the mockery and ridicule of passengers from front and behind. Piccadilly Circus would turn into a real circus: people shouting, car horns honking, and the two of us trapped in that bubble – and Mansi wrapped in his fits of laughter!

4

Our apartment at Thurloe Place, opposite the Victoria and Albert Museum, opened onto an alleyway that led to the luxurious house where Margot Fonteyn, the great ballet dancer, lived with her husband, the Ambassador of Panama. It was a spacious apartment, which I shared with Salah Ahmed Mohammed Salih, and on his departure to Sudan with Mohammed Ibrahim al-Shoush. The landlord, Mr Bomberg, a brother of the renowned painter David Bomberg, visited us occasionally – late in the evening with his wife – and we would spend hours talking art, poetry, literature, theatre, politics and a host of other topics that appealed to people in the prime of youth, carefree, and eager to make the most out of life.

Unfortunately, I did not buy that apartment, although Mr Bomberg had generously offered it to me at a very low price in appreciation of our lovely evening chats. That was one of many wrong decisions I made and precious opportunities I failed to take advantage of.

Now, as my remaining life is getting shorter and the shade

of the past is growing longer, I look back only to see those mistakes as high as mountains on the skyline. Mansi laughed at me: "You will always remain the dunce you are. How could you miss such an opportunity?"

Perhaps he was right, who else other than a dunce like me would pay the bills of a millionaire like Mansi, as I did during our stay in Sydney?

I would see Margot Fonteyn being driven back and forth in her Rolls Royce and we would exchange greetings from a distance. It took me two years – and a trip to Damascus – to get closer and talk to her face to face. As for Mansi, no sooner had he found out she lived next door than he introduced himself to her and her husband; in no time, they became friends, exchanging visits. He also made the acquaintance of the renowned Australian actor Peter Finch and the famous British actor Peter O'Toole, who both lived near him in Chelsea, then a favourite place for artists, writers and actors.

When house rents soared in the 1970s, many of the residents there moved further out to east and north London, while others headed even further away, deep into the country. It was not difficult for Mansi to penetrate that attractive community, which by its nature was open, less intolerant to outsiders than other English communities. But even if this had not been the case, would that have deterred Mansi? No way. Anyhow, he was now perfectly armed. Besides his audacious character and strong command of the English language, he was now living in a famous street, in a select district, blessed with noble in-laws and a wife who was a famous pianist. Strangely enough, Mary did not seem to be terribly interested in the arts community and she did not have the typical artists' aura. Rather, she looked more like an ordinary housewife, always seen sweeping, washing or cooking. Mansi, in contrast, always occupied centre stage, talking ceaselessly about virtually anything: painting, poetry, theatre, music – you name it.

Through these strong connections, he found minor roles in films. The way he described a part would give anyone the impression he was playing the leading role. Yet on watching the film, we would see him in very marginal bit parts – a taxi driver in Cairo or a waiter in a Beirut café – lasting no more than a minute or two. Had he had the slightest acting talent, these connections could certainly have taken him to stardom. He was definitely a talented actor on life's stage, but in art, it was a different story. Once placed in front of a microphone or camera, he would become ridiculously shy or over-react.

Gamal al-Kinani, the late head of drama at the BBC, used to favour Mansi with a role in every play he directed, and enjoyed teasing him. Everyone savoured hurling abuse at him. Al-Kinani would yell: "You son of a . . . How come you keep jumping and dancing around and once the red light is on, you die away? Damn you! Why can't you apply some of this mischief of yours to work?"

But Mansi could not; for real life is one thing and art is a different matter. Mischief can work in real life but never in art. In real life, he was a born artist, as if supported by invisible forces. He took risks, overcame barriers and transcended the set boundaries, like a gifted poet. If he had resigned himself to the role life had set for him, he might have achieved much more. I have no doubt that, had he wished, he could have become a business tycoon. But Mansi wanted to live and write and act – and above all, laugh. That was his greatest passion: turning his life events into a subject for laughter. His happiest moment was surely when he sat at the centre with people around him listening attentively to his stories. That was his real theatre. It would be best if there were someone like me who had been witness to those events in order to refresh his memory and keep his excitement high.

"Tell them, Tayeb, when we went to Beirut, what happened at the airport?" With that he wanted me just to give the lead for him to relate the full story all by himself, my role being to add a small remark every now and then and direct the conversation back to the course he wanted to follow. So apart from being a godfather to him, I played a secondary role like those one sees in such comedy duos as Laurel and Hardy, and Morecambe and Wise. In such shows, you see two characters sharply contrasted in physical appearance and mental qualities: lean versus fat, tall versus short, someone smart and resourceful getting out of trouble unscathed versus a stuttering and stumbling dunce, always taking the brunt. The latter was my role – a role, let me admit, that I took consciously of my own free will.

Apart from the strong affection I held for him, Mansi was an extraordinary phenomenon I was keen to observe. Monitoring him was a source of confusion, astonishment, some-times annoyance, yet keeping his company was often a source of pleasure. In fact, all his close friends felt the same; I just might be the only one amongst them who had accepted Mansi the way he was and taken him seriously.

But Mansi himself did not take seriously the role that life had set for him, and tried to play roles he was not prepared for. When he committed a mistake in life, it would be because he behaved as an artist in a real-time setting, becoming like an actor on the stage who forgot his words and ended up stuttering, losing the ability to reciprocate. Thus, he settled for a few millions instead of billions, for a single palace rather than many palaces, yachts, private jets, banks and companies. Now he has died like a racehorse that had fallen before the finishing line, I feel he was a wise man, an ascetic to some extent. What would a dead man lose if he left nothing behind? And what benefit would he get if what he left were a million or a billion?

All the plays he had written, except for a few, were rejected. I remember a particular one that he wrote about a man who comes across another man trying to commit suicide by throwing himself off the top of a bridge into a river. After a long conversation, he manages to convince the desperate man that it is not a good idea. However, as soon as the latter leaves, the other man commits suicide himself by jumping into the river. Mansi was quite excited about his play but on reading it, I found it dull and lifeless. It was obvious that he was influenced by the great playwright Samuel Beckett. But it didn't carry the faintest glimmer of

Beckett's thought and philosophy and I had to reject it.

It was a big surprise to learn later that Mansi had presented an English translation of the same play to no less than Samuel Beckett himself and that the great writer whose famous work *Waiting for Godot* was a breakthrough in international drama, read it carefully, discussed it at length with Mansi and praised it as a beautiful, interesting piece of work.

5

Had it not been for Mansi, may God rest his soul in peace, things would have continued to run perfectly in my favour at the BBC. I was happy, and so were my superiors who often cited me as a role model. I was not yet thirty when they promoted me to the position of assistant department head, a rare occurrence at the time. As a result, I found myself attending meetings of heads of departments, and I had my own office and a secretary.

I even attended the Queen's coronation ceremony at Westminster Abbey, and I found myself side by side with VIPs from around the globe. I later sat with heads of state and prime ministers at the party held at the Westminster Hall. It is true that the costume I wore for the occasion had been rented from Moss Bros in Covent Garden: a black suit with a long tail that made me look like a penguin, a top hat and a starched collar. But it is also true that when the party was over, chauffeur-driven cars came in to pick up the heads of state and prime ministers while I walked down to the underground station.

The tube was so crowded I had to stand up, and people kept staring at a man dressed like a noble amongst the masses. That odd situation would have fitted Mansi better. He would have exploited it in the best way and turned it into an exciting story. I, for one, enjoyed that fantasy world for a day that was too short; little did I know that life was flirting with me, as always, like an attractive lady, trying to coax me into doing something that had never crossed my mind.

Also, I was the first Arab to be sent to New York to cover the meetings of the UN General Assembly, an event that brought together most of the world's leaders. I was there when Nikita Khrushchev banged the table with his shoe in protest while Britain's Prime Minister was delivering his speech. I saw members of the Nigerian delegation jubilantly enter the hall in their flowing attire, led by the venerable Sir Abubakar Tafawa Balewa. Nigeria had just gained independence and become a UN member, before it was brutally destroyed and the venerable Ahmadu Bello was slain in one of those rash military rages called revolutions.

I was there when Dag Hammarskjöld, the UN Secretary General, announced that he was not succumbing to the Soviet Union's calls for him to resign. Years later, the United States did the same thing, exerting pressure on my friend Amadou-Mahtar M'Bow, UNESCO Director General. In New York, Khrushchev launched a tirade against Hammarskjöld, describing him as a lackey of the West and holding him accountable for the Congo tragedies. I still remember a phrase of Hammarskjöld's short address announcing that he was staying in his position. Addressing Third World leaders, he said: "This organisation has not been established to serve the superpowers. It has been established to serve you, for it's you, not the superpowers, who need it."

At that meeting, the Arabs were unanimous on two things: Rallying behind the Palestinian cause and supporting the Algerians' struggle for independence, which was coming to fruition. They were at odds on everything else.

But I was too young. And so was the Arab world. Egypt and Syria were united under one flag. Damascus was truly glorious and open-handed. Cairo was giving birth to dreams that seemed very much attainable. Salah Jaheen was writing and Umm Kulthoum was singing – and so was Abdel Wahab. Sabah's chant, "I know my way, from al-Moski all the way down to al-Hamidiyah Souq", sounded as if she literally meant it. Poor old Hamidiyah Souq! At the time it was still there by the Great Umayyad Mosque of Damascus, as it had been back in the days of Caliph Hisham ibn Abd al-Malik. They had not yet demolished that historical monument and run asphalted roads through it.

And Lebanon was living a seemingly endless romantic dream. Money poured in from all corners, as the Arab poet said – "The house is flooded down to the estuary that is Lebanon". Banks did not have enough room to keep cash. The lira was as strong as gold and people thronged restaurants and nightclubs from sunset to dawn. The ladies of Beirut would stay on at the Corniche to greet the Mediterranean sun – as if that pleasant time was meant to last forever. Our brother Nizar Qabbani's romantic poems would cause young girls to wet their velvet pillows with tears and would stir old women's yearnings for a youthful time that would never be re-visited.

September is the season for romance,
So take me in your arms,
And let us embrace.
Did they tell Mother I am here with you?

Oh! Look, folks, how life has played havoc with you and me ever since?

Yes, they were truly generous to me. They dispatched me on prolonged assignments to the Beirut office, a privilege only a few enjoyed. I lectured at the training institute several times. Mr Waterfield, our senior manager, once said to me humorously: "They have invited me only once. How come they keep inviting you time and again?"

My share of business trips was clearly greater compared to others. In most cases, my name automatically popped up as the favoured nominee for challenging assignments that most likely weighed heavily in annual reports.

No wonder, then, that I was elated, self-satisfied, seeing life as a charming lady waiting for the faintest hint from me to come to my side.

In the midst of all that, Mansi, may God rest his soul in peace, abruptly intercepted my path just as Satan had done to Adam in Paradise.

6

I entered Mr Waterfield's office. He was sitting with his assistant and the controller of foreign broadcasting services. The latter was a dreadful man who would come our way only when something serious happened. We were not best friends; he believed that I was given an easy ride as one who paid little heed to internal administrative policies. Mr Waterfield did not smile at me as usual; he gestured for me to sit down. The controller gave me a sharp look from behind his thick glasses, and without uttering a single word, handed me a bundle of papers. I flipped through them; they were payment orders in the name of Mr Bastawrous on account of his participation in a number of programmes. They were all signed by me. Having noticed nothing unusual, I returned the bundle to him. Once again, he returned it to me. "Check the papers, carefully," he said.

I started to study them more carefully as I racked my brain for an explanation for what was obviously an administrative trial over a serious matter. Apart from the senior official, a secretary sat in the corner, taking minutes. This time too, I could not detect any irregularities. I raised my head and looked at him; my look must have betrayed my feelings about him because Mr Waterfield, who was always kind to me, gave me a light smile as if to say "Be patient".

Mr Waterfield, as I told you earlier, was a writer and the post of head of the Arabic Service was too junior for him. Deep in his heart, he detested bureaucracy and rigid administrative rules and had waged several battles against this man in particular.

The controller said to me in a cold tone, as perfectly cool as the English tone would sound when it lacked cordiality: "These signatures here are yours, aren't they?"

"Yes, they are."

"Did you check the papers carefully?"

"Yes, I did."

"Did you notice any irregularities?"

"What do you mean by 'irregularities'?"

"The remuneration, for instance."

"What about the remuneration?"

"How much would you pay a grade-A actor for taking part in a 30-minute play?"

"We would pay x amount."

"And if that actor is a BBC member of staff?"

"We pay one third the standard remuneration."

"See the amounts paid to Mr Bastawrous." He handed me the papers again.

Looking again, it was full pay.

"Were you aware that Mr Bastawrous – or Mr Ahmed, or whatever his name – was a BBC member of staff, working as an editor in the Foreign Broadcast Monitoring Unit in Caversham?

I kept silent as I started to realise the grave mistake I had committed. I cursed Mansi secretly. But I did not give it much thought. I was too young, too inexperienced. Perhaps I said to myself: "If this *khawaja*[4] is arrogant, I should outdo him in arrogance. Worst case scenario, I will resign and go back to where I have come from, and rid myself of all these contradictions and heartache. So I decided to stand up to that challenge as "a true Arab" would do when things got really rough.

"Yes," I said.

Suddenly, the assistant head of department turned to me and repeated the question, cynically and slowly: "Were you aware that Mr Bastawrous was a BBC member of staff, working as an editor in the Foreign Broadcast Monitoring Unit in Caversham?

This *khawaja,* too, was not one of my best friends. At its best, our relationship fluctuated; improving sometimes, plummeting most of the time. He was not one of the "Pro-Arabs" like Mr Waterfield and Mr Whitehead, those men and women who had spent their youthful years in the Arab world and had known the Arabs in and out and loved them. This one was a specialist in German affairs, a brilliant man with a brilliant academic record to his credit. It seemed, though, that he had experienced some difficult circumstances that played havoc with his life. He had worked

---

4 A nickname for a European

largely in the East European broadcasting service, which we considered more relevant to the Foreign Office than to the BBC. At that time, we the Arabs, supported by Mr Waterfield and Mr Whitehead, fought hard to keep the Arabic service away from the yoke of the Foreign Office, and to make it a proper broadcasting service.

He was mired in contradictions and provocative, would induce you into discussion but once you spoke your mind he would show you his hostile face. He would always present himself as a liberal and would tell his Arab visitors: "I am a radical thinker, affiliated to the fundamentalist left wing of the Labour Party." My comment on this was always: "Mr X claims he is a liberal when he is actually an imperial colonialist." That comment apparently annoyed him, for he summoned me one day to his office and said: "You are causing me tremendous embarrassment with what you are saying." Drawing on the English "rules of the game", I said: "But Mr ... it was just a joke. Can't you take jokes? Don't you English people claim that you outsmart all other nations with your sense of humour?"

I can see now that I was too indifferent at the time – perhaps I was self-conscious of the delicate position I was in, particularly during those years of heightened sensations of nationalism that were sweeping the Arab world. It was as if any career success I achieved with the British would further complicate my position. I was like one bent on demolishing what he himself had built the day before. No one could appreciate, or tolerate, that attitude except great people like Mr Waterfield and Mr Whitehead.

"Yes," I said.

They looked at each other in a way that only later would I understand.

"And was Mr Kinani aware of this?" asked the controller, with a false tone of kindness, thinking that he had led me into his trap.

Gamal al-Kinani, may God rest his soul in peace, was the most senior Arab in the department at the time, enjoying a free hand with the full support of Mr Waterfield and Mr Whitehead. No wonder, the controller hated him more than me, and it was obvious he wanted to kill two birds with one stone.

"I don't know."

"How come?" Aren't you his assistant who takes charge in his absence? Haven't you discussed this?"

"No."

They looked at each other again. The assistant department head said to me in his usual unkind tone: "Mr Bastawrous is your friend, isn't he?"

At this point, Mr Whitefield came to my rescue. "Take it easy," he said to his assistant, giving him a stern look.

7

I wish I were a servant of Sayyidina Abdullahi ibn Omar holding his camel's rein. It was reported that a man hurled abuse at him while he was walking on the road. Sayyidina Abdullahi went ahead silently but the man followed him with successive curses. Only upon arriving home did Abdullahi turn to the man. "You Mr," he said, "my brother Asim and I do not hurl abuse at others."

What strikes me most about this story is that he said "My brother Asim and I . . ." He clearly did not want to attribute all the credit to himself or it could be that he mentioned his brother in this context out of deep affection for him. Asim, as we know, was to become the grandfather of Omar ibn Abd al-Aziz, the grandson of that Bedouin lady who had refused to adulterate milk and said to her mother: "If the Caliph can't see us, surely God can." On hearing that, the Caliph Omar ibn al-Khattab selected her as wife for his son, Asim; one of their descendants was Omar ibn Abd al-Aziz (Bani Marwan) who filled the land with justice during his short-lived reign.

For even though I was not known to be a curse hurler or troublemaker, Mansi drove me to the point of losing my temper that day. He interrupted my life to tarnish my fancy dream. Now I was accused of administrative delinquency, an accusation that hardly needed substantiation but was nonetheless tolerable. What was not was that my personal integrity, hitherto beyond suspicion, was now at stake.

"Mr Bastawrous is your friend, isn't he?" asked the assistant department head. Although Mr Waterfield kindly came to my rescue, the damage had already been inflicted: an accusation, true or false, had been made against me.

Even worse, I came to know later that they had interrogated the department head, Gamal al-Kinani, ahead of me. Despite his maturity and long experience, he committed a grave mistake: he said he was not aware that Mansi was employed in another BBC department. All the department executives denied any knowledge, which meant that I was the only one who had taken a different course. That annoyed them. I acknowledged the accusation of delinquency, putting myself under suspicion.

That was why I lost my temper and hurled abuse at Mansi as much as my disposition allowed me. But he did not take me seriously and regarded the whole matter as a joke and mischief. As usual, he had embarrassed a huge, sophisticated administrative system. Payment orders would be sent from us to the administration unit for review and audit. From there they would pass on to the administrative unit of foreign broadcasting service and on to the central administrative organ. Mansi, may God bestow His mercy on his soul, worked in the broadcasting monitoring unit under the name of Michael, and with us under the name of Bastawrous. At the same time, he worked as English language teacher in a high school under the name of Joseph. For almost three years, that situation continued undiscovered despite a succession of administrators and auditors – until the matter was discovered by mere chance. In recalling this story, what interested him most was that he had been teaching the British their own language.

How could he do these jobs simultaneously? Using his bubble, he would shuttle back and forth between places far apart. At one point he would be seen in Caversham, an hour's drive from London, before suddenly popping up on the extreme north of the city, and then with us at Bush House. No wonder all the department executives denied any knowledge: they truly were not aware – but at the same time they were aware. And I cannot say for sure whether I adopted a contradictory story in order to protect Mansi or because it occurred to me that I had been aware.

It took me considerable time and effort to redress my mistake. And I never managed to regain that favourable stature I had enjoyed, as that incident continued to blemish my annual appraisal reports for quite a long time. Mansi, on the other hand, came out of it unscathed. He had managed to get to the Director of External Broadcasting, the number two man in the BBC, second only to the Director General. He forced his way into Mr Tangye Lean's office without prior appointment. The moment he introduced himself, the man let out a loud guffaw. As Mansi told us later, the man said to him, between giggles: "So, you are the man who put the Arabic Service in big trouble!"

Tangye Lean was one of the 'great' men – the calibre of Mr Waterfield. He was by no means a strict bureaucrat, but rather tolerant and farsighted. He was an enlightened person who had spent part of his life in Egypt. And he was a prominent author: he wrote an important book, entitled *The Napoleonists: A study in political disaffection, 1760–1960*, about the Britons who had swum against the nationalist current in Britain and sided with Napoleon in his struggle against England. He had strong connections with writers and artists: his brother, David Lean, was the renowned director of *Lawrence of Arabia*. He must have been impressed by Mansi, for they soon became close friends and he invited Mansi to his home and introduced him to his family. Shortly after that, Mansi was reinstated in his position at Caversham, and the Arabic Service was instructed to lift the ban off him.

Mansi remained close to him until his death. He returned the favour when Mr Tangye Lean visited Egypt. Mansi, who at the time was a lecturer at the American University in Cairo, devoted all his influence and connections to serve his guest. He accorded him a prime minister's welcome and arranged for a private jet to fly him to Luxor and Aswan, and personally escorted him on all his tours.

I would see Mr Tangye Lean only once every year, when he would read my annual appraisal report to me. When he reached the sentence that had become a permanent comment in my reports over many years, ". . . but he needs to give more attention to administrative matters", he would put on a kind smile, as if to say, "Don't worry, I know where this accusation has come from".

8

It was through Mrs Barbara Bray that Mansi, with all his noise and clamour, managed to storm into Samuel Beckett's serene, exclusive world. The playwright and novelist whose works were celebrated as masterpieces and landmarks in world literature had been living in France, inaccessible except to a close circle of disciples and friends. No statements to the press; no TV interviews. And when he won the Nobel Prize, he shouted in panic: "Now the curse has befallen me." He kept himself out of sight until the commotion subsided. A few years back, I had thought I should interview him for *Hiwar* [Dialogue], the renowned literary magazine edited by Tawfiq Sayegh. When I asked Mrs Bray to arrange a meeting for me, she said: "I will. But when you meet Sam, you will realise that you shouldn't have insisted on interviewing him."

"Sam," she explained, "is a saint, an introvert absorbed in his own world and thoughts, has little interest in world affairs; wants to be left alone."

I respected his wish and never tried to see him again.

Avoiding interaction with people might sound weird coming from a writer whose works seemed to lament that man was haunted by a compulsive tendency to shun socialising and lead a lonely life. Was it because he had grown up a Catholic before breaking away afterwards? Or was it because he had been a close friend of James Joyce, the great Irish writer, author of *Ulysses*, who could be credited with setting off the first revolution in 20th-century literature?

Beckett had taken from Joyce his great attention to the language, as well as his absurd lifestyle. Yet he eventually broke away from the influence of his master and set a unique course for himself, presenting a shocking artistic image of Man all alone in a desolate desert, engulfed in global darkness. He was a writer who attached more attention to pauses between sentences than to sentences themselves. No wonder he entrusted his plays only to directors whom he trusted, and he often insisted on directing them himself. He continued to make his writings more concise and compact, deleting words and adding more silence, to the point of reducing one of his most recent works, which he called "A novel", to a one pager.

Such was the world that Mansi stormed into, with all his noise, fuss and hilarity – a world in sharp contrast to his own (but was it really so?). His means to that was Mrs Barbara Bray.

This lady was one of the most kind-hearted people I have ever come across. It was Mansi who introduced me to her, around 1954. She was head of the script unit in the BBC domestic broadcasting department. Of course, it hadn't taken Mansi long to discover the presence at the BBC of the lady who had taught him English language at the University of Alexandria. If I was a godfather to him, this lady was no less than a godmother. It was a truly moving relationship. With her, Mansi would be himself, laughing like a child, telling her all the tiny trivial details of his life, and she would laugh, rarely finding anything odd in what he said or did. Mansi kept in touch with her, calling her up from wherever he happened to be, and stopping over in Paris to spend a day or two with her after she went to live there.

Barbara had graduated in the late 1940s from Cambridge University where she studied English literature. She and her husband lectured at Alexandria University for some time. Her husband, a gifted poet, died in a car accident in Greece, leaving her alone to deal with bringing up their two daughters. The eldest studied Chinese Language and became one of very few Chinese Studies scholars. The younger specialised, and excelled, in Arabic language. To Barbara goes most of the credit for discovering names such as Harold Pinter, John Arden, and John Osborne, who were later to become icons of English theatre. Taking advantage of her position as head of the script unit, she promoted their works, even adapting some for broadcasting on the Third Programme [the present Radio 3].

Certainly, Samuel Beckett had her to thank for his popularity in England. Beckett was already well known in Europe, particularly in France, for he wrote in French as proficiently as he did in English. The Germans, too, loved him because they found the gloominess that pervaded his works particularly appealing. The French liked him for his linguistic adventures and great talent – which he shared with Irish writers in general – in blurring the boundaries between seriousness and jest and pushing things beyond the bounds of reason. As for the English, the Anglo-Saxons, they had to wait until the early 1950s for people like Barbara to step in and help them discover the genius world of this unrivalled writer.

9

Surprisingly, that great writer did find in Mansi someone who could capture his attention to the point where he would regularly devote an hour or two to him. Soon, Mansi would refer to him as merely Sam, as if they were intimate friends.

What did Samuel Beckett find in Mansi? They seemed to be polar opposites. The former was a man who led an ascetic life, peering into the fathomless depths of his soul and enduring tormenting spiritual and mental pains. All these had left their mark on his sharp features and tired face, grooved as if time had been drilling through it with a sharp tool. His eyes shone with focused looks, a mixture of challenge and panic – as if staring at something horrific that no one but him could see. Before him, writers, poets, painters, and philosophers, had peered into the same gaping abyss: some committed suicide; some went insane, while others pursued other courses to lead themselves out of that dilemma. But this man chose the same stormy course that the blind poet Abu al-'Ala' al-Ma'arri had taken: he took the toughest of courses, living in isolation, totally devoted to his intellectual and spiritual preoccupations.

In contrast, Mansi, it seemed, lived at the edge of life, running from one experience to another, always seen chattering and laughing, showing a high profile wherever he went.

Beckett must have spent part of his time listening to Mansi. And he must have resigned himself to the role of listener, for Mansi would never give anyone, even Beckett, the chance to speak. Also, he must have read Mansi's writings, and he might have found in them something attractive, just as great painters would sometimes find appealing features in children's drawings. Furthermore, it may be that the writer who weighed his words admired the audacity of a man who would readily say anything that might cross his mind.

Luckily for Beckett, Mansi would descend on Paris as swiftly and briefly as a hurricane: a day or two and he would be gone. And as Beckett spent most of the time in the countryside, their meetings were infrequent. However, Mansi always kept in touch with Barbara Bray. In fact, he would go to Paris specifically to see her. He would ring her from Washington, London, Cairo, Riyadh, or wherever he happened to be, and all of a sudden he would be at her doorstep – and she was always there waiting for him, as a mother patiently waiting for her child. Whenever I happened to be in Paris, I would attend these encounters. Mansi would be truly himself, totally at ease, laughing and chattering while she and I would listen, and I would take my usual supporting role, prompting him when his memory failed him, completing a sentence or giving him the lead in to a story. Barbara would listen, her face radiating with great affection. After making her shy, refined laugh, she would say: "You and Mansi should do some comedy stage show together."

"Like Laurel and Hardy?" I would say.

"Or Abbott and Costello," Mansi would add.

Each time we met she would take us to a new restaurant in that Paris suburb that was as familiar to her as her palm: small restaurants, cheap yet not frequented by tourists, each specializing in a particular dish. During our last meeting, we went to a restaurant on the Left Bank that specialised in fish and oysters. Mansi came with his Arab Muslim wife, carrying his son, Abdulaziz, on his shoulders. He had named him after Sheikh Abdulaziz al-Tuwaijri, who had taken good care of Mansi during his stay in Riyadh. That night, Mansi told us how he had made a profit out of that marriage. Sheikh Abdulaziz had taken it upon himself to cover all the expenses. Not only that, he had booked a hotel suite for the bride and groom and given Mansi some pocket money, but when it was time to leave the house and go to the hotel, Mansi was nowhere to be found. A search was made and he was found sound asleep in one of the bedrooms.

When he decided to propose to his wife-to-be, her family set him an appointment and explained to him how to get to their house. But he went to the wrong address and had to wait a long time before a member of that family found him sitting there and asked him who he was and what it was he wanted. Mansi responded with a question: "But where are the others?"

"What others?"

"Is this not the house of . . . ?"

Meanwhile, his in-laws-to-be were waiting at their house. They had almost lost hope and were about to leave when he finally reached them.

It was time to pay the bill, and Barbara wanted to settle it. It was always either she or I who paid, while Mansi would look on as we argued about it – as if it were not his call to pay. He was by no means a miser, however. In fact, he could be very generous sometimes. It was only that with certain people, he would take the role of one who took but never gave – as if it was his chosen way of demonstrating his affection for them. But this time I was adamant that Mansi must pay. Quoting Abdel Raheem El Refaie's description of Mansi, I said to Barbara: "This mule is a wealthy man. He came to Paris in a long American limousine and is staying in a five-star hotel. The price of this fur overcoat alone can meet your needs for an entire month. Why should you or I pay? We are both poor."

"Stop this fuss," Mansi said. "Either you pay or let Barbara pay."

His wife, who apparently had not yet known him well enough, was embarrassed. "Ahmed, please pay."

"Ok," he said. "If I had known it was going to fall on me, I would have made cheaper orders."

When he died, I waited for some time to pass before calling Barbara, afraid she may not have heard, and knowing how devastating the news would be to her. But I found out that she had already heard the news, yet she sounded more heart-broken than I had expected.

Towards the end of the phone conversation, she said: "Of course, you are going to write about Mansi."

"He and I had agreed to co-write the story of his life: in English, then in Arabic," I replied.

"It would have been a very important book, a bestseller too. Mansi was an important and a rare man, in his own way."

"Now that he's gone, I don't know. There are incidents that I am not aware of. There are things that would have been better told by him, in his own way. But I will think it over. Perhaps I will write about him, but after some time."

10

On our way to London University Students' Union, Mansi asked me to brief him on the Palestinian question.

It was a bold decision on the part of the Students' Union to select such a topic for debate in those tense days of the early 1960s that "This Council is in favour of the establishment of an independent state for the Palestinians in Palestine".

I have no idea who selected Mansi as the main defender of the Palestinian cause that night, against such a staunch opponent as Mr Richard Crossman. It must have been his passion for debate and for the limelight that had thrust him forward for the role.

"Richard Crossman? Who cares?"

But Richard Crossman was such a formidable opponent that anyone, other than Mansi, would have been on their guard if they were having to face him in debate. He was a top-notch leftist thinker and a prominent theorist for the Labour Party. He had taught at Oxford before becoming a member of parliament. Later he served as minister and a bona fide advisor to Prime Minister Harold Wilson. Upon leaving his cabinet post, he became editor of the highly influential *New Statesman* magazine. He had served on an ad hoc committee set up by the British Government to study the conditions of Arabs and Jews in Palestine, and he was utterly biased to the Zionist side.

Less than an hour before the beginning of the debate, while travelling in that same bubble car of his to the venue, Mansi said to me: "Hey! Tell me quickly this story of Palestine."

"You mean to say you are going to face Richard Crossman so unprepared? Don't you know who Richard Crossman is?"

"Stop the fussing. Just tell me quickly about this Balfour Declaration and all that nonsense."

"But this is no joke. This is a very important debate, a rare opportunity that will not come again. I wonder who selected a fool like you to be a spokesperson for the Arabs."

"None of your business. Just give me some brief information. Don't worry about me. Richard Crossman or whoever else – who cares?"

I was truly alarmed. The hall was thronging with people – and those who could not find seats stood in the lobby and gangways. There were Arab and foreign ambassadors, MPs, journalists, photographers, radio and TV crew – It was evident that both sides, the Arabs and the Jews, had worked hard to mobilize people. That came as no surprise, for debates organized by university student unions, particularly in Oxford and London, had a profound impact and often attracted media attention.

Fortunately, Mansi had a strong team. One of them, I recall, was Erskine Childers, a journalist who was a staunch defender of the Arabs and the Palestinian cause in particular, although he was to back off in the face of mounting pressure, and vanish altogether.

As Mansi walked up to the podium, his short figure protruding at his behind and his belly, he was greeted with a strong wave of applause from the Arab side. That must have provided him with extra courage. He talked confidently, in eloquent English, though he said nothing particularly interesting. He tried to conceal his ignorance by saying that he would leave it for his team to give the details.

Fortunately, each member of his team was well prepared, and they all delivered informative presentations supported with irrefutable facts.

The coordinator then gave the floor to Richard Crossman, a tall man who walked to the podium to a storm of applause from supporters, including many who were neither Arabs nor Jews but merely fans of Richard Crossman.

He spoke in his usual hoarse voice and unique style: a combination of the solemnity of a former Oxford professor and the cunning of a veteran politician who had learnt the craft from Labour Party congresses and House of Commons battles against heavyweight opponents such as Winston Churchill and Antony Eden. What on earth could our poor knight do with this monster? Once Richard Crossman stepped down, I had no doubt that the Palestinian cause had been dealt a painful blow that night.

Yet something very strange happened after that. I cannot recall exactly how it happened, but I do remember seeing that giant monster of Zionism retract in size, his mouth opening and shutting as if he had lost the ability to talk, his face reddened, and his forehead covered with sweat. Our knight, Mansi, transformed into a voracious monster, running back and forth between the rear of the hall and the podium, making hand gestures towards the man's throat and almost thrusting his finger into his eye.

"Tell me: are you British or Israeli?"

Richard Crossman's face got even redder, and our friend Mansi kept running gracefully down the hall and bouncing back to the podium like an arrow, turning his eyes, now dilated to the maximum, around the hall. It seemed as if some energy from an unknown source had descended on him.

"We know you are Jewish. We have no problem with that. Everyone has the right to be whatever he wants to be. We are not against Jewish people. But we need to know: Who are you paying allegiance to: Britain or Israel?

Richard Crossman was not Jewish, to the best of my knowledge, but it was obvious that Mansi was deliberately trying to cast doubt on his credibility and strip him of the veil of solemnity and respectability that shrouded him. And he did that with great success, turning the debate into a farce and his opponent into an object of ridicule.

When the votes were finally counted, it turned out, to our surprise, that the motion our poor knight stood for emerged victorious, although he was no more knowledgeable on the Palestinian cause than a camel herder in the deserts of Kordofan. That victory served to strengthen Mansi's long-held conviction: that honesty, logic and straightforwardness hardly lead anywhere; what is more effective in life, whether it is the Palestinian cause or anything else, is bluffing.

Thanks to that debate, Mansi attracted the attention of many, including President Abdel Nasser himself, to whom the Egyptian Embassy, according to Mansi, sent a full report supported by photographs, describing how a young Egyptian had humiliated one of Britain's greatest politicians. Mansi's story was probably true, for soon after that he received an invitation to a conference of Egyptian expatriates. That ushered in a new phase in his life. But before that, he committed perhaps the boldest act in his whole life that nearly led to his expulsion from Britain.

11

As I came out of the gates of Bush House, to make my way to Paddington station for a train to Oxford, Mansi appeared before me: "Tayeb! Where are you going?"

"Oxford?

"Oxford? What for?"

"Professor Toynbee is delivering a lecture on the Palestinian question."

"Palestine again? Why don't you stay in London? The weekend is approaching."

"But this is a very important lecture."

"OK, I will go with you."

I laughed. That was typical of him: once he discovered that I was heading anywhere he would instantly say "I am coming with you". That was how he accompanied me as far as India and Australia.

"You are just a homeless wanderer. Why don't you just go to your wife and kids?"

"Wife and kids? Come on! Give me a break. Let's go!"

He was truly blessed to have married such a kind lady as

Mary. Though he had a wife and children, he continued to lead a carefree life as if he were still a bachelor. He would travel and return, appear and disappear, and she would never grumble – as if he were a guest.

Sometimes I would suddenly remember that I had not seen him for two or three weeks and I would reach for the phone. And Mary would say: "Mansi's not here."

"Where is he?"

"I don't know."

"How long has he been gone?"

"Two weeks."

"Don't you ask him where he's going?"

"You know Mansi. That's how he is. But he always comes back."

After her tragic death in a fire accident at their Washington home, he remained faithful to her memory, describing her as a saint. I am a witness to how close to the truth that description is.

"Forget about the train. Let's take my car."

"No way. I am not going all the way to Oxford in that lousy car of yours! And you call it a car?"

"Are you still in the age of the bubble? We're in a new stage now, boy. I've bought an elegant car – it's truly luxurious!"

That turned out to be no more than a second-hand car – I cannot even remember the make – which he had procured in his crooked way: his friend the butcher knew someone who knew a garage owner who knew a used car dealer.

"But I enjoy travelling on the train."

If I had the authority, I would have connected the entire Arab world – from Tangiers to Muscat, and from Lattakia to Nyala – with a railway network such as the TGV high-speed trains in France and the bullet train in Japan. To those who used to travel for a month or two on camels' backs from Sana'a to Mecca, the abrupt jump to this crazy means of transport would seem insane. Airports, no matter how advanced they have become, always seem temporary. But railway stations have their own flavour and charm: remote stations and changing sceneries; you know you have left one place and arrived at another; you sleep and read and meet different people. Unlike the plane, where in a twinkling of an eye, you are in a completely different world.

"Forget it. Hurry up. We don't want to miss the lecture."

He reversed roles as usual: Now it looked as if it were he who was going to Oxford, while I was his companion, not the other way round.

Halfway to Oxford, he said: "I have a friend here. Let's call on him for five minutes."

"Who's he?"

"A senior executive at Arthur Rank."

"We should rather push on. The lecture is at 7 pm."

"They're producing a film about Lawrence. Guess who is playing the part of Lawrence – Alec Guinness. The co-star role will be a young Arab. They're considering Omar Sharif and I want to snatch it from him. The director is David Lean, Tangye's brother. Tangye promised to recommend me to him."

I laughed but remained silent.

"Why are you laughing? You think Omar Sharif is better than me?"

"No. No. Who said Omar Sharif is better than you?"

"If it comes to fluency in English, I am thousands of times better than him."

"Certainly."

"And if it comes to acting skills, my performance has won the admiration of Laurence Olivier."

"Amazing!"

"You don't believe me, do you? Did you know who taught Laurence Olivier how to play the part of the Mahdi in the film *Khartoum*?"

"You?"

"Yes, me! Believe it or not! The man was stunned when I recited all the Hamlet monologues from memory, in exactly the same way he did in the film."

"Stop it, son. This is not a joke. Bluff games can work in anything except in art. You have a good command of English and you know the monologues of *Hamlet* and *Richard III* by heart. But you are a lousy actor. Omar Sharif is an international actor – but who are you? Who has heard of Mansi Bastawrous? Even your name is not attractive enough for cinema. Besides, Omar Sharif is a handsome man, while you are . . ."

"And, am I not handsome? Girls say I look like Aly Khan. Even Princess Margaret was attracted to me at that Buckingham Palace party."

"Have you met Princess Margaret?"

"Of course I have. Come on! You know the whole story!"

The mere act of recalling that story was a source of great joy to him and he burst into that same laughter of his. I laughed too, albeit for a different reason, for I knew they had almost expelled him that night.

We arrived at a huge house overlooking a beautiful valley, where we met an Englishman who looked as though he belonged to a different era. Although we had come without prior notice, he was truly happy to see Mansi.

"Michael! What a pleasant surprise! How amazing! I was just thinking about you!"

"I decided to drop by, on my way to Oxford to attend an important lecture by Professor Toynbee. Oh, I forgot to introduce my friend, Mr Salih – he works for the BBC."

The man turned to me: "Ah. So you work with Michael?"

"Yes. Mr Michael, as you know, is a senior executive in the BBC. He is my direct superior."

Mansi could not conceal his delight at seeing me take on the role satisfactorily, and as if he wanted to return the favour, he said: "Mr Salih is one of my most competent aides."

The man then devoted himself totally to Mansi and I was able to figure out from their conversation why he had been thinking of Mansi and why he was so happy to see him.

12

Mansi was laughing as usual as the man from Arthur Rank stood at the gate of his house, waving us goodbye.

The car went along the road and headed towards our destination. It was a second-hand car – true! And God only knows how Mansi acquired it – true! But it was a car that had windows and doors, and could travel at a speed of 200 kilometres per hour.

In a way, Mansi's life can be compared to the types of cars he either purchased or acquired like a gift from the heavens. In the latter part of his life, when he became Master of Tatchbury – or Lord Tatchbury, as he used to say – living in the palace that he claimed had been King John's hunting lodge, he would go out every morning in knight's attire, on his horse Sam, ride past his grazing cattle and sheep, and inspect his oak, pine, apple and mulberry and strawberry trees. His neighbour to the east was Lord Mountbatten, an uncle of Prince Philip, the Duke of Edinburgh. His neighbour on the west was Lady So-and-So. Arriving at the stables, he would walk about talking to the horses, patting their necks and inhaling the unique smell that horses have.

Visiting the garages was the last leg of his tour. There he would open the doors and the cars would be lined up like the horses in the stables. He would inspect them one by one, lifting open the bonnets, opening the doors and getting in. He would sit there, hands on the steering wheel and take off on an imagined drive while the car stood motionless. The Ford, the Rover, the Buick, the Jaguar, the Mercedes, and finally, the Rolls: he would lift each bonnet as a groom would lift the veil of his pretty bride. He would get in and fill his lungs with the aroma of that fantastic leather smell. He would hold the steering wheel, turn the engine on, then off. He would then get out and go and stand at the edge of the nearby pool and watch his image as it dispersed and came together, and as it grew longer and then shorter on the water's surface. Only a few people could walk barefoot or ride a donkey or camel and still look out at the horizon as haughtily and proudly as a prince. Actually, Mansi was approaching the finishing line, and it was as if he found no reason to lengthen his journey.

But let me not get ahead of myself. We are now at the beginning of the journey, on the road to Oxford, in a car that has windows and doors, and enough room for you to stretch your legs. And you can open the window if you wish, and inhale the refreshing air of the English country-side. On both sides, lush fields undulate like folds of a dress, and Anglo-Saxon villages with their stone buildings and slate roofs nestle in the valleys and hillsides. We left the English man from Arthur Rank standing at the gate of his home waving to us, his eyes beaming with a dream that would never come true, just as Mansi's dream of getting Omar Sharif's part in *Lawrence of Arabia* would never materialise.

Although I had overheard part of the story from Mansi's conversation with his English friend, I opted not to ask him about it now as we headed to Oxford. I would rather leave it to sink in and take shape in his imagination. I would often witness an event with Mansi, only to hear him later relating a story completely different from what I had seen and heard.

We were received on arrival in Oxford by Karrar Ahmed Karrar and Hassan Bashir.

"Who is this *halabi* you've brought along with you?" Karrar asked me, looking at Mansi.

Out of affection, we call our Egyptian brothers *halab*, or gypsies – and out of affection too, they call us other names.

"*Halabi*?" Mansi bounced back as if he were an old acquaintance of the man. "You think I am one of those Egyptians from *Wajh Bahri*[5]? I am in fact a *saeedi*, closer to you."

The late Karrar, may God rest his soul in peace, was a typical Sudanese, embodying all the merits – and some of the disadvantages – of a typical Sudanese. He was the epitome of a 'Bedouin chief', as we say. Even here in Oxford, dressed in his western style suit, he looked as if he were wrapped

---

5 The delta region of Egypt

in that traditional flowing thobe, holding a stick, and sitting under a big tree, surrounded by his tribesmen. A career administrator, he served as inspector and district commissioner during British rule, and after Independence rose to the position of governor. Other posts included assistant secretary general of the Council of Ministers in Sadiq al-Mahdi's first cabinet, and Minister for Cabinet Affairs during Nimeiri's regime. He was an expert on Southern Sudan, but that did not deter Mansi from getting into a heated debate with him about South Sudan, a topic he was as knowledgeable about as he was about the Palestinian cause.

Hassan Bashir, on the other hand, was a friend and classmate of mine. He had worked at the Ministry of Finance and later served as assistant governor of the Central Bank. He could have advanced even more, if he was not too straightforward to win favour with his superiors.

13

We sat in the first row. No wonder the hall was full; the lecturer was Arnold Toynbee, the greatest historian of his time. Besides, the event per se was one of a kind; a historical occasion, if I may say so. Both the Arab Students Union and the Jewish Students Union at Oxford University had extended a separate invitation to Professor Toynbee to deliver a lecture on the Palestinian question. The old man said he was not fit enough to deliver two separate lectures but would be happy to give one speech to a combined house of Arabs and Jews. The Jewish students accepted without hesitation. That was typical of Jewish people in general; they would not miss a chance to reach out to Arabs. As for the Arabs, some refused outright while others appeared hesitant.

Things have changed now.

Back in those days, contacting Jewish people or the mere act of talking to any was almost taboo for Arabs. It was a weird scene back then when an Arab and a Jewish person were invited, among others, to one of those talk shows on a European TV channel. The Arab would adamantly refuse to sit with the Jewish person in the same area, so the hosts would put him in a separate room and would spend most of the time grilling him on why he refused to sit with him. Consequently, the Jewish person would appear the winner without having made much effort. Only a few Arabs were courageous enough to challenge that taboo.

At that young age, we had strong temptation to challenge those taboos. "Don't we have brains as they do, and stronger arguments than theirs?" we would say.

I remember a colleague at the University of London, an English girl of Jewish origin. I still remember her name after all these years – Shirley. She had a pretty face, cheerful eyes, and dimples in her cheeks that played havoc with our hearts when she laughed. There were five of us: from Egypt, Iraq, Palestine, Morocco and Sudan. And Shirley was always in our company, preferring us to others, and always asking us why Arabs and Jews couldn't live together in peace. And we would say: "Yes, for God's sake, why not?" She would say: "We are cousins and most closely related," and we would reply: "You're right: Arabs are the descendants of Ishmael, son of Abraham, and Jews are the descendants of Isaac, son of Abraham."

Arabic and Hebrew have so much in common. You are right, Shirley. They have so much in common.

So why the war and bloodshed? Why the squandering of energy and money? Why can't peace reign over these territories? And we would say to her: "Why not, indeed?"

Each one of us, let me confess, was perfectly prepared, if he had the choice, to sign a unilateral peace treaty with

Shirley.

One morning she walked up to us, like that Japanese girl had walked up to her Egyptian boyfriend in the famous poem by Hafez Ibrahim. "It's time to bid you farewell," she said.

"Farewell? Why, Shirley? Where are you heading off to?"

She looked at us astonished for a moment before answering our question in the same way as the Japanese girl had answered her Egyptian boyfriend:

She said in an alarming tone,
Sounding not the gazelle I've known,
Rather a dreadful lion:
"I have to leave now,
Unlikely to return."

"But why?"

Looking at us again, with eyes that were not cheerful, and cheeks that had no dimples, she said: "Didn't you know that war has broken out between Egypt and Israel?"

We replied as the Egyptian had said to his Japanese girl-friend:

I said in pain and despair:
What on earth would gazelles do at war?

We said to her: "What have you got to do with war?"

She said: "I am a soldier in the Israeli Reserve Army and I have been called up."

We looked at each other, and each one of us conducted a long silent talk with himself as well as with the others: is it conceivable that this sweet girl would go to war, carry weapons, fight with enemies and kill Arabs?

Our confusion then transformed into a fierce rage: at ourselves, at Shirley, and at Israel.

Being in the prime of youth, we had great capability for forgiveness and great aptitude for sacrifice – but no one had called on us.

We, along with scores of Arab youth, went down to the Egyptian Embassy offering to volunteer. They said to us: "God bless you. We will call you if we need you. But for now, the Egyptian army is very much in control."

But, on looking at TV screens, we saw Israeli soldiers bathing in the Suez Canal.

It is true that the British and the French had come to Israel's aid in that 1956 war, and the same scenario repeated itself during the 1967 war.

As for Shirley, she never came back; maybe she killed or was killed; maybe she decided to stay permanently in Israel.

What a strange time that was!

14

No wonder the hall was full, for the speaker was no less than Professor Arnold Toynbee, the greatest historian of his time, the most far-sighted and the most knowledgeable. He was a historian who perceived human history as a rough sea, a wave rising to a peak then subsiding before another wave comes up. Successions of civilizations are born; they grow and prosper and then wither and die, giving way to new ones.

We sat in the first row. Mansi was restless. He kept turning his head right and left, smiling at whoever his eyes fell upon. He was clearly refreshed by the Oxford air, and his soul had succumbed to the magnetic power of that charming place. This small town, which derives its character and spirit from its famous university, is in fact a symbol for the best and worst of British 'civilization'. To Britons, graduating from here was proof of association with the privileged elite. Heads of students' unions in Oxford most likely rose to seats in Parliament, probably to the premiership. At the peak of the British Empire's might, Britons in their twenties, with nothing unique about them except that they belonged to the ruling elite, went out from this tiny place to control the fates of nations such as India, Sudan, Nigeria, Kenya and Palestine; each one of them ruled a land larger than the British Isles.

To Mansi, Oxford University was an unfulfilled dream, an English fort that he had not yet invaded. That was why his face lit up and his glances from one side to the other grew more frequent once the college towers appeared on the skyline. We drove past buildings whose architecture carried echoes of churches and medieval castles, while the thick walls, the huge doors, the rectangular windows and the internal courtyards must have been borrowed from Arab Andalusian architecture. Mansi kept reciting the names of colleges as though he were chanting an ancient mythical song – Balliol, Merton, Magdalen, Wadham, Keble – and throwing his smiles left and right, particularly at girls trotting out of lecture rooms or cycling past on their bikes. Occasionally we would come across a lecturer rushing past; his black gown billowing in the air.

Toynbee looked around the crowded hall, his face radiated with an enigmatic smile as he turned his shining eyes towards the faces of the audience, Arabs and Jews.

The Arab and Jewish students were seated under one roof for the first time in Oxford University. The late Karrar was one of those who convinced the Arab students to attend. He was a student leader; he and Hassan Bashir were postgraduate students at St Antony's College.

Toynbee's speech was full of knowledge and wisdom. I

remember him saying that the story of the Arabs and Jews in Palestine resembled the Greek epic tragedies: malicious acts one leading to the other in an endless circle. He talked at length about the atrocities in Europe against Jews – in Russia, Italy, France, Germany and England. He talked about the suffering of Jews at the hands of the Nazis in Germany. He said that those heinous acts, unprecedented in human history, could not be simply attributed to the act of one insane person – Adolf Hitler. Rather, he said, it was a sin that the whole of Western European civilisation shared accountability for.

On the other hand, Toynbee talked extensively about the tolerance that Jews had found from Arabs and Muslims, particularly in Andalusia, where the Arab-Islamic civilisation had allowed Jews there to realise their full potential; many of them became ministers, ambassadors, scientists and philosophers. He was surprised that Jews who had suffered incredible torments at the hands of the Europeans could deliver the same persecution to other people who were not responsible for their suffering. He concluded by calling on both parties to break that vicious circle and break away from what was a historical impasse. Otherwise, he said, it would inevitably lead to a catastrophe that would affect the whole of mankind, just as had happened in the Greek tragedies. He made a special appeal to Jews to work courageously and boldly to probe another non-violent path away from that historical stand-off.

Most of the applause was more out of courtesy than heart-felt support, for Toynbee's address was too balanced and too decent to find favour with either side. Arabs, in those critical times, would accept nothing less than unequivocal support for their cause, while Jewish people were too self-conceited to see themselves at fault. But this was an address from a man who had pondered extensively on the fates of people and nations, and perceived, more than any other historian of his time, mankind's passage since the dawn of history as a well-integrated chronicle. Being almost eighty, it mattered little to him to placate either side, the Arabs or the Jews.

The hall went into a deep silence, like the one that reigns when people hear something totally unexpected.

And from the womb of that silence, sprang Mansi, like a stone thrown into a still lagoon.

15

Mansi turned his back to Professor Toynbee and rolled his eyes over the silent audience who turned their attention to the standing figure. He inserted his left hand in his pocket, inflated his chest, and raised his head. Slowly, he started to turn towards Professor Toynbee while the left half of his face was still leaning towards the audience. He took a dramatic posture, perhaps inspired by the image of Laurence Olivier, acting as King Henry V, urging his soldiers to fight the French in the Battle of Agincourt. He had memorised most of King Henry's speeches in that Shakespeare play, and would recite them in a voice almost identical to Laurence Olivier's. Or perhaps he was imitating Napoleon at the Battle of Austerlitz. Dreams of grandeur did cross his mind occasionally, but they soon faded away like a passing summer cloud, leaving hardly any traces behind. He was at least as tall as Napoleon. His posture there carried a faint – very faint – resemblance to Napoleon's posture in David's famous painting. This ancient place, Oxford, is replete with history and illusions, with dreams that had dissipated like a passing summer cloud, and dreams that had come true. A bit of this must have hit Mansi and forced him to behave in that awkward way.

He spoke in an excessively overacted way, stressing 'Professor' and 'Toynbee', which he pronounced 'Ta Anbee' in the style of English aristocrats:

"Proffffesor Ta Anbee: I listened attentively to your valuable lecture and found in it a lot of things worthy of contemplation. But let me first thank you very much in my own name and on behalf of all those present and I believe I speak for all of them when I say it was a highly valuable, highly informative lecture. However, let me say that I was truly surprised to hear a historian like you, a great historian like you, who was not known to be anti-Arab – in fact, we the Arabs, consider you a friend. Yes, I was truly surprised to hear you say that the Arabs had, throughout history, mistreated the Jews; persecuted them; tortured them . . ."

I was sitting on his right, with Karrar and Hassan Bashir on his left. The three of us simultaneously looked at him in panic. There was murmuring among the audience, as well as some muffled giggles, and I kept tugging at the tail of his suit attempting to force him to sit down; but he had transmigrated into another state, into a dream that was difficult to drag him out of.

"And you are saying Arabs now have to help Jews out of this historical impasse that they led them into. Who put Jews in a historical impasse, Professor? Was it not you, Europeans?

You were the ones who persecuted them and hanged them in public squares. And you are saying Arabs are still hanging the remaining Jews in public squares. This is pure fabrication and false Zionist propaganda.

"You were the ones who did that; placing them in detention camps and in gas ovens. Now you want us Arabs, who hold no guilt for what happened to Jews, to make amends for your sins, or in your words, Professor, to break the vicious circle that you Europeans created. No, sir. Palestine is an Arab land. It had been so for ... for ... three thousand years ... And it will remain an Arab land forever. We will take it back by force, sooner or ..."

The murmurs developed into clamour, and loud voices in Arabic and English could be heard all over the hall, asking him to sit down. When I finally managed to pull him down into his seat, he said: "What? Did I say something wrong?"

"Just shut up, fool. I will tell you later."

The respectable scholar looked deeply perplexed. And for the rest of the night, as he answered questions, he kept glancing at Mansi from time to time, as if trying to solve a riddle. In his humbleness, typical of great scholars, he must have thought that he might have misrepresented his thoughts; otherwise, how could he have been so awfully misinterpreted? As for Mansi, he sat quietly and confidently as if he had done nothing wrong.

As we went out, Karrar, who had now taken to Mansi as if they were old friends, said to him: "You *saeedi* idiot: apparently the Egyptians of Cairo are right. It seems true that a *saeedi* was fooled into buying the tram. Were you out of your senses or were you sleep-walking in another world?"

Laughing in his attractive, childish way, Mansi said in a theatrical *saeedi* dialect mimicking Egyptian films: "Honestly, your lecturer took too long. And I was terribly exhausted as – forgive me for saying this – I had a lovely night yesterday in London. And today I drove all the way to Oxford – so I did fall asleep."

"Besides," he added, "we are fed up with this Palestine issue."

Hassan Bashir interrupted: "So when you were too exhausted and sleepy to follow the speech, why couldn't you just shut up, instead of this tirade – as if you were Gamal Abdel Nasser? I was under the impression you were about to say: 'What has been taken by force must return by force.'"

"Believe it or not, it was on the tip of my tongue, but this guy here kept pulling me down by my jacket, and I had no idea why he was doing so – I was even surprised that people didn't applaud me."

I was sure he had selected the figure 3,000 randomly, so I said, in an attempt to tease him: "Who told you Palestine had been an Arab land for only 3,000 years?"

"For how many years, then?"

"At least 7,000 years."

"Is that so? I thought it was 3,000 years. Jews are saying it has been their land for 3,000 years, so I said to myself: make it 3,000 also – not bad. Is 3,000 years not long enough, folks?"

16

At Oxford, Mansi was like a fish in water, or more accurately, like a wild zebra in the wilderness. We made the acquaintance of so many. At St. Antony's, the college of Karrar and Hassan Bashir, we met the sociology scholars – the Lienhardt brothers, and the man who translated *Doctor Zhivago*, the famous novel by the renowned Russian writer Boris Pasternak, from Russian. It was later made into a film starring Omar Sharif, Mansi's 'competitor' in *Lawrence of Arabia*, who played Doctor Zhivago. We also met the renowned English writer John Wain, who was at the time a professor of poetry, a position that Oxford had created to honour writers and poets.

Mansi was totally at ease in that open, enlightened world, where people spoke their mind and played with ideas like ping pong balls. He would take part in any discussion, whatever the subject, no matter how well or little informed he was about it – be it sociology, economics, philosophy, politics or literature. Sometimes he hit the mark, sometimes his shots went wide; but he always made up for his ignorance with his excellent command of the language, cheerfulness and good sense of humour. No wonder he left a good impression on all those he met. He enjoyed the time there so much so that he wanted to stay longer, encouraged by Karrar, who liked his cheerfulness and prattle. But I put my foot down.

"This man is an idle wanderer. I have got to get back to my work," I told them.

"What work, smartie? You call what you are doing work?" Mansi sprung back.

Mansi never took broadcasting as a serious job, describing it as a facile game, a profession that required no prior knowledge or effort. Yet he loved it, and when he migrated to the USA, he established a broadcasting station to propagate Islam – by then he had converted and become a devout Muslim.

That cheerful mood that had overwhelmed him during our stay in Oxford continued to linger as we drove back to London. He continued to laugh and chatter, jumping from one topic to another and from one idea to another, hardly following any logical order. Little by little, his 'scene' with Professor Toynbee started to evolve in his mind as another episode in his myth-rich life. Letting out one of those laughs that came from the depth of his heart, he said: "Imagine: I attacked the man without knowing what he had said."

"Your foolish acts at Oxford have cancelled out your London victory over Richard Crossman – like Napoleon, who gave away in Moscow all he had gained at Austerlitz," I said.

He liked the analogy with Napoleon.

"Am I truly like Napoleon?"

I burst into laughter.

"Why are you laughing? Who's Napoleon after all? An obscure Italian from Corsica!"

"But who are you really like? Aly Khan? Napoleon? Who else?"

Jumping to another idea, he said: "You know something? Gamal Abdel Nasser is truly a brave boy, a courageous *saeedi*. But unfortunately he is surrounded by an ignorant bunch. Do you know what kind of people he should have taken as consultants?"

"People like you!"

"Exactly! One like me – *saeedi*, courageous, well educated, well versed in crafty games – who can play smartly with both eggs and stones!"

I laughed at his comment as much as I did when he had compared himself with Napoleon.

"You're laughing again? Do you think those nobodies around him are better than me?"

"D'you know them?"

"Of course I do. You know that guy – what's his name? – he's now a senior minister. His wife used to have her dresses made by the Greek woman who was my landlady in Alexandria. He used to come with her. We became acquaintances and then close friends, spending evenings together."

Later, when Mansi returned to Egypt and lived there for a while, he claimed to have made the acquaintance of

Gamal Abdel Nasser and become one of his advisors, writing summaries of newly published English books for him. That was a claim we never took seriously.

I had deliberately brought Mansi back to Oxford.

"Oxford is lovely, isn't it?" I said.

"Oh, what a place! You know I registered for a PhD at Oxford?"

"You're kidding!"

"Didn't you know that? I very nearly married a pretty girl from Oxford. She was studying history at St. Hilda's."

"And then?"

"Then what? You know the rest. I stumbled on you – and on the BBC, started playing some rubbish scripts and getting paid."

"And you got married to Mary."

"Yes, sir."

"Mary is a decent woman. You don't deserve her. Anyone in her place would have divorced you a long time ago."

"I can't dispute that. Mary is a kind lady, a good housewife and all that rubbish. But the Oxford girl was very pretty, a peach."

I remembered his friend from Arthur Rank, so I asked about him and Mansi responded instantly to this new topic as if he had long been waiting for that prod.

He said laughing: "The fool you saw earlier holds a senior position in the company. He's from a prominent family and is married to a beautiful lady."

"I thought he was not married. It didn't look like there was a lady in the house."

"That's the point. He went to Egypt where he met a young Egyptian girl, 22 or 23 years old. He was captivated by her beautiful eyes, black hair and sexy body, and he felt crazy about her. What a fool! He was over fifty."

"And then?"

"And then what? The girl was not serious. She deceived him and made him believe that she loved him and would marry him."

"Did you meet her?"

"Of course I did. I've been a witness to this story from the very beginning."

Then he added: "You don't seem to notice. I am working with them as Arab affairs advisor – so when they want to produce a film such as *Khartoum*, *Lawrence of Arabia* and this rubbish, who would they consult?"

"You?"

"Of course, me! You think I am surviving on this BBC rubbish?"

"Then what happened?"

"Just like a typical English man, when this stupid *khawaja* returned home, he told his wife that he intended to divorce her, saying he was in love with another woman. How weird? His wife was extremely beautiful!"

"Don't tell me the girl was Muslim."

"No, sir. Don't worry! She was Coptic – I know her family. You remember that you are Muslim only when it comes to marriage. Even if she were Muslim, this man was prepared to do everything in his power in order to marry his sweetheart."

"And the girl?"

"Come on! She's cheating him! She will never marry him!"

"So why are you interested in this matter?"

"Believe it or not, this idiot would call me at 2 am to tell me about his love affair. He believes I can convince the girl to marry him."

"In return for what?"

"Now you're getting to the point – in return for helping me snatch the role from – guess who? – Omar Sharif!"

"Damn you! You will ruin his marriage!"

"No. Nothing like that will happen. He will go back to his wife eventually and that will be the end of the story."

The actual end of the story: the man from Arthur Rank neither divorced his wife nor married that girl. And Mansi took neither Omar Sharif's role nor any other role in *Lawrence of Arabia*. Yet Life still had some other real life roles in store for him.

17

When Mansi made his new 'historic' scene, in a place that was not particularly accessible to everyone, he might have felt that he was there in response to some fair logic, that he too stood for something. He was in stage two of his life: the "bubble" stage that followed the "bicycle" stage.

It was in the late 1950s, or perhaps the early 60s – I cannot remember exactly. But it was a grand event. The British House of Commons played host in London to the Conference of World Parliaments. Delegates came from all parts of the world and it happened that Mansi had been a close friend of the head of the Egyptian delegation as they had been students together at the University of Alexandria. So it was easy for Mansi to spend a lot of time with the Egyptian delegation. He would accompany them around town, assist with their shopping, arrange their meetings, escort them to clinics, and facilitate everything for them. As one might imagine, he made use of his incredible energy and thorough knowledge of London. He soon became indispensable and little by little it appeared as if he were one of them – a member of the delegation. He later told me that he had duped the conference secretariat into putting his name on the list of delegates. So he started receiving all the conference papers, including invitations to the parties thrown in their honour. Soon, Mansi would attend the conference sessions during the day and receptions in the evenings. The Egyptian delegation did not see anything odd in that as they thought he was representing the BBC.

So Mansi had found a decent role that befitted him, and he engaged himself fully with it. And as was his habit when he was absorbed in a role, he knew no limits.

However, an incident occurred that nearly had him deported from Britain.

Everything was going perfectly well, until the evening when the Queen hosted a farewell party at Buckingham Palace in honour of the delegations. Mansi dressed in a dinner suit that he must have rented or borrowed, and then headed to the Palace, a place more charming, glittering and solemn than all the places he had been to. I can imagine how Mansi entered Buckingham Palace, that imperialist stronghold steeped in protocol and ceremonies.

I remember when he accompanied me once to a reception at an embassy; of course, he had not been invited, but he came nevertheless – as if he believed he had a standing invitation to every single function held for any reason whatsoever, anywhere in the world; as if he considered himself a permanent guest at life's table. At the door had stood a man in a smart red jacket, looking like an army general, who called out the names of guests, one by one, as they stepped into the hall. I did not like that, saying to myself: "What's the point of all this?" So I went in without giving my name. After a short while, I heard the gatekeeper calling out in his strong voice: "Dr Michael Bastawrous, head of the BBC Arabic Service." The real head of the BBC Arabic Service, who happened to be present, looked around in astonishment.

Yes, I can imagine how Mansi managed to penetrate that well-fortified stronghold which was not particularly accessible to everyone. He must have passed through the perimeter iron railings that tourists hang on to as they watch the changing of the guard ceremony, hoping to catch a glimpse of a face looking out from a window. He must have entered into the internal courtyard, and might have ventured upstairs before doors were opened and the royal guard led him through long and broad corridors; each step had been meticulously measured since time immemorial. Finally, he must have reached the ultimate destination.

And there he arrived, without permission or authorisation, in a borrowed suit and under false pretences.

The last door opened, and the Queen's gatekeeper, who was certainly unlike any other, called out: "Dr Mansi Yousif Bastawrous, head of the Egyptian delegation."

Do you remember him as he battled with Sir Antony Eden at the Young Conservatives meeting? Do you remember him knocking down one of the gigantic British dragons? Do you remember him at Oxford, waging a meaningless war, a meaningless battle?

Yet here, in this very place, he was playing a part that was greater than any he had played in the past or would play in future.

In his borrowed costume and false identity, Mansi stood before the superior symbol of the British Empire, the Queen of England, Scotland, Northern Ireland, Wales, the Hebrides and the Isle of Man, heir to the throne of Kings James, George and Edward, a descendant of the Houses of Windsor and Hanover, Head of the Church, Head of the Commonwealth.

So how did Mansi react? Did he greet and leave? No way. That was a moment he must have been unconsciously bracing himself for since birth, as if fate had prepared him for that 'historic' meeting. Perhaps he became certain that he too stood for something; he didn't go there as a beggar; rather, his stance there was in response to a certain rationale that, though appearing strange, was, in a way, quite fair.

18

The head of the delegation was too sick to attend, Mansi came to know, and there was no one to act on his behalf. That must have been inevitable – a twist of fate; for the same strange rationale that had bestowed 'legitimacy' upon Mansi and provided him, consciously or unconsciously, with justifications for his conduct, now dictated that he, and no one else, should play that role and act as the delegation head.

Why not?

Hadn't Napoleon, an obscure Italian from Corsica, snatched the crown, placed it on his own head and declared himself Emperor of France?

Doesn't life liberally bestow its bounties on certain people who do not seem to have any advantages over others?

Don't some people occupy more space than they deserve?

By the force of that strange rationale, Mansi stood, along with heads of delegations, in the line leading up to the Queen, the imperial icon for whom the royal anthem was played, and in whose name armies marched and flags fluttered on tops of warships on the high seas.

Behind him in the line was Mohammed Ahmed Mahgoub, head of Sudan's delegation. That too was fair in a way: that Mohammed Ahmed Mahgoub, with all his lofty stature, stately appearance, eloquence, superb mental power, and experience in politics, should stand behind Mansi, in his borrowed suit and false identity!

Years later, we related that incident to the late Mohammed Ahmed Mahgoub, may God rest his soul in peace. At first, the leader in him was annoyed, but when he recalled the poet in him, he laughed. Perhaps by then he was more able to see the 'moral' of the story more vividly: he was in exile in London, after 'the victorious May Revolution' had pushed him out of the premiership. Someone, who was in the end no different from Mansi, had jumped in (without authority and under false pretences), and driven him out and planted himself in his place.

Heads of delegations greeted the Queen, who would say a few courtesy words to each one before they moved on. This would last no more than a minute or two.

But Mansi was different. He was not commissioned by anyone; he came on his own accord, not as an intruder, but rather by the force of a rationale that he considered fair – and in whose name?

In the name of all those who stood behind the railings looking on from a distance in the hope that a face would look out of a window. In the name of those who could not find a place on the table because others had occupied more space than they were entitled to.

According to Mansi, may God rest his soul in peace, after the Queen had greeted him as per protocol, he blurted out, without even calling her 'Your Majesty' as that protocol dictated: "Listen, you must be finding these occasions excessively boring. How can you tolerate this tedious job day after day?"

Mansi claims that the Queen laughed, but most probably she put on a thin smile to conceal her surprise at his waywardness. She is properly accomplished in dealing with such scenarios.

He then had a lengthy talk with her about her functions as Queen, and about her family life, and was bold enough to ask about the upbringing and education of Crown Prince Charles. As if that was not enough, he went even further to give her guidelines on the best methods for the Prince's upbringing and education.

The encounter took too long. The line came to a halt and heads of delegation began to wonder who it was that the Queen had gracefully allocated all this time to. Behind Mansi stood Mohammed Ahmed Mahgoub, waiting for his turn, with all his lofty stature, long experience, and elegant suit that was surely his own, not a borrowed one!

The Duke of Edinburgh, who was standing beside the Queen, stepped forward, gently took Mansi's arm and led him out of the line. "You are pretty young," he said to him, "too young to lead the delegation of a great country like Egypt."

Mansi spent that evening as one would expect: eating and drinking, discussing, arguing, and laughing, making the acquaintance of Lord X and Lady Y, showing off in his impeccable English in the heart of Britain's strongest fortress. Yet, in the midst of that pleasure, he forgot something crucial: that the palace was not an unguarded space, and that no one can get into that fortress without invitation or authorisation, irrespective of whether he felt he represented something or had some right. Vigilant eyes were there, watching and guarding, seeing and hearing.

The next morning, in the early hours, he had hardly risen from his bed, when well-built men, the likes of whom he had never seen before, descended on him. Security authorities were aware of every tiny detail about him since he had first set foot on their island – every tiny detail was documented. And over a month or so, they kept tightening the rope around his neck, accusing him of acting as an agent for Egyptian intelligence – they said they could not find any other plausible explanation for his suspicious behaviour. Strangely enough, the Egyptians too accused him of being a spy – working for British intelligence – they too found his behaviour dubious.

So Mansi found himself in a serious dilemma that required all his energy and connections to extract himself from. Ultimately, the British came to the conclusion that he was either an idiot or insane, and not accountable for his behaviour.

But Mansi, may God rest his soul in peace, was neither an idiot nor insane. He was, as his teacher Barbara Bray proclaimed, "a rare man in his own way".

19

In Cairo, a conversation one evening with our hosts – the famous playwright Saad Eddin Wahba, who held the post of Under-Secretary of the Ministry of Culture at the time, and his wife, the great actress Samiha Ayoub – covered diverse topics. Then Mansi's name was mentioned. Saad Eddin Wahba began to tell us about a trip he had made to Kuwait, accompanied by Mansi. So I was not the only one who had the pleasure of travelling in Mansi's company, though I could be the most privileged.

Mansi, may God rest his soul in peace, had a strong passion for travel; he established a tourist company that gave him the advantage of discounted air travel and hotel accommodation. He loved company and laughter. If he discovered that a friend was travelling anywhere, he would join him without hesitation. He had a profound love for Salah Jaheen; if he thought of him while he was in Washington, he would instantly fly all the way to Cairo to see him. If he thought of Abdel Raheem El Refaie, he would fly to Bern; and if he thought of Barbara Bray, he would fly to Paris. He was a free man, free as a bird.

Before Saad Eddin Wahba could continue with his story, the doorbell rang. It was our friend, in flesh and blood – as if he had showed up in response to an invitation. Coincidence? Yes, but one that repeated itself many times: his name would be mentioned, when no one knew he was in town, and suddenly we would hear a knock on the door or the ring of a telephone.

He came in, laughing, as if he had been in our company for some time.

"Mansi! Curse you! Where the hell have you come from?"

They hugged him and showered him with kisses and curses – particularly curses, for there was something in him that tempted others to hurl curses at him – in jest, of course.

His face beamed with joy at the warm reception and strong flow of curses, and the dramatic impact of his entry into a house whose owners were much better versed in drama than he was. He found himself being dragged from right to left by people who knew and loved him to varying degrees: Yusuf Idris, Mahmoud Salem, Ragaa El Naggash, Abdel Moneim Selim, and others.

He joined in the conversation as if he had been present from the very beginning, and he obviously enjoyed the evening, having found a unique audience who were truly gifted, entertaining, with a great sense of humour. He put on the clown's costume and soon became the focus of attention.

Saad Eddin Wahba went on with his story, frequently

interrupted by 'the star' in an attempt to drive the narration on a course he preferred. I was not giving full attention to the story; little did I know that I was soon to take up a role in one of its miserable episodes in Beirut.

Mansi was fond of engulfing himself in mysterious surroundings; appearing suddenly out of nowhere and disappearing just as abruptly.

"What awful wind has brought you here?"

"And why do you want to know?"

Yusuf Idris, who had long been fascinated by Mansi's character, said: "This guy must be a CIA agent, otherwise, how could he possibly know we were sitting here?"

Mansi would only laugh; he loved to lend more mystery to himself.

Someone else added: "I am not sure the CIA are stupid enough to employ such an idiot, one whose entire life is jest and jokes and can't keep any secret."

"This is camouflage," a third suggested.

The truth of the matter was far simpler, however. As Mansi told me later, in a more serious setting, he had arrived from the US two weeks before and had visited relatives in Cairo and in Upper Egypt and checked on his sisters and brothers – something he did regularly. Then he disappeared for several days in the company of his close friend Salah Jaheen before popping up that night.

It had been more than fifteen years since he emigrated to the US. When we were together in London, I would tell him: "Go to the US; it's a land where you can either go to jail or become a millionaire."

But he did not take me seriously for he was happy in England. Then, one day, in his usual way, without any prior plans, he went on one of those trips to New York arranged by the BBC where participants could pay a small amount to cover the airfare and accommodation in New York for a week.

He went there without any intention of staying; he had not taken much money or personal belongings. Besides, his visa did not permit him to stay. Yet everyone returned except him. His companions said he had vanished upon arrival in New York and they had no clue as to where he had gone.

20

That day, at Cairo Airport, I should have paid more attention as we completed departure formalities. I did catch a glimpse of Mansi running back and forth, whispering in the ear of the airline staff, mumbling to the customs officer, and chatting with the passports officer. But I said to myself: "This is how Mansi is – turning anything, no matter how simple and straightforward, to near conspiracy." Even as we climbed up the steps into the plane, I saw him whispering to the airline staff, but none of this stirred my curiosity. He was cheerful as he entered the plane, as if he had achieved some sort of victory.

We arrived at Beirut Airport in the early evening. It was the day, in 1975, that was to mark the actual beginning of the Lebanese Civil War, the war that has not come to a halt till this day. We arrived just ahead of the beginning of this farce, to a loaded atmosphere in an evening that was a prelude to a long, dark night that concealed appalling tragedies.

The previous evening, at Saad Eddin Wahba's house, Mansi had asked me about my travel plans. I told him I was heading back to Doha where I worked, but was going to stop over in Beirut for a couple of days.

I had been attending a meeting of the permanent Media Committee at the Arab League Headquarters. We discussed issues that were to become the agenda of all Media Committee meetings and Information Ministers' conferences until this day: Arab media strategy abroad, the negative image of Arabs in Western media, the creation of an all-Arab news agency, the endorsement of a media code of conduct, stopping inter-Arab media propaganda, and other topics. It was a respected committee that comprised highly esteemed gentlemen: Sa'adoun al-Jassim, Ali Shommo, Ghalib Abul Faraj, Ibrahim El-Salahi, Abd al-Aziz al-Rawwas, Mursi Saadaddin, Abdullah al-Horani, Gumaa al-Fazani, Sheikh Isa bin Salman, Taha Yassin, Adeeb Yassin, and others no less kind and wise than those mentioned. They were all men of reason and wisdom. That was a time that called for a great deal of reason and wisdom; I am not sure if this is still the case now.

We used to say: "Let us focus on the permanent objectives of the Arab Nation and avoid being caught in temporary, short-lived issues." We were trying to establish a solid platform in an ocean of moving sands. That committee, to the best of my knowledge, was the first to coin the phrase 'minimum Arab consensus', a phrase that was to acquire greater dimensions later on, when echoed at higher levels. Fortunately, most of the committee members remained on board for four or five years so a close affinity developed between them. Even our brother Gumaa al-Fazani eventually embraced a 'realistic and professional' approach, as we used to say.

Meanwhile, our tolerant chief, Dr. Abdul Ahad Gamaluddin, kept using his good offices to put off revolts and extinguish fires, and when things got too complicated he would resort to his innate Egyptian sense of humour and say something that would send people into fits of laughter and all the tension would dissipate. To his right sat Saleem al-Yafi, the assistant Secretary General, listening silently, suffering patiently, and smoking ceaselessly.

We visited the Secretary General, who was in hospital. He was quite warm and hospitable and we chatted about many issues and when the conversation moved on to media issues, he said: "What media? What I want to create is development!"

"But, Your Excellency," one of us said, "isn't media part and parcel of development?"

That was the last meeting of the permanent Media Committee to be held in Cairo; after that, much water flowed under the bridge and people went their own different ways.

"A great idea," Mansi said, "going to Beirut. I was planning to go to Riyadh. Great! I will spend a couple of days in Beirut after which you go to Doha and I proceed to Riyadh."

One hour was enough to take someone from Cairo to Beirut; the same distance between Cairo and Aswan – and Damascus is even closer to Cairo than Aswan is, imagine!

The plane flew over Beirut in the early evening. The mountains, the sky and the sea looked exactly as had been described by the poets in their poems, and by Wadih El Safi and Fairouz in their songs. Peace, love and tolerance: that was what Lebanon really stood for. Ironically, everything was perfectly set for destruction. Hundreds of thousands of men and women had worked tirelessly over decades to build a country only to offer it ceremoniously – like a bride – to death.

But little did we know about that on that evening of 1975.

21

The sky over Beirut was clement and clear, close at hand; its stars looked like pearl necklaces blending with glittering electricity lamps at the base of mountains. To the left, as the plane approached the airport, was a sea that looked soft and transparent in that early part of the evening; its waves, that looked like brides dressed in white, were crashing on the shore where they dissolved. Shortly, that clement sky was to shower flames, those luminous mountains were to shake under the thundering of machine guns, and this peaceful sea was to send out demons of destruction onto its shoreline.

We entered the arrivals terminal and proceeded to the baggage claim hall, little did we know that all the above was impending.

All of a sudden, I came to my senses, as if I had woken up from a dream. I said to Mansi in a terrified voice: "What's this, you idiot!"

"It's nothing. A few gifts," he said.

"What gifts? These are smuggled goods."

Some gentlemen from the Qatari Embassy had come to receive me. They entered the customs area and stood there looking on, perplexed.

Porters carried in two huge boxes, each maybe weighing tons, and when the customs officer insisted on checking their contents, Mansi said: "Why the trouble? These are just small gifts." Then he added, insensitive to the presence of the Qataris: "Besides, I am an official representative of the State of Qatar, and a member of an official delegation."

The Qatari Embassy officials turned startled, curious eyes on me, but I was more astonished than they were. I had seen countless examples of Mansi's audacity but it never crossed my mind that it would take him to the point of falsely claiming that he was an employee of a country when their embassy staff were physically present. As always, my feelings were a mixture of anger and embarrassment but also intellectual curiosity, as if I were engrossed in watching an attractive artwork unfolding before me. So, suddenly, that part of the airport turned into a theatre, and we all – members of the Qatari Embassy staff, the customs officer, a number of people drawn to the scene, and myself – were transformed into a chorus in a comedy in which Mansi was playing the leading role.

The customs officer insisted that the two boxes be opened; they looked suspicious, particularly at a time of high tension, as we later came to know. They could contain arms, drugs, or any other banned items, who knows? So the covers were lifted, and we looked in: the boxes were full of ladies' lingerie, of all makes and colours. The officer was busy emptying the boxes, and as each bundle was taken out, my anger, embarrassment and perplexity soared.

Mansi, meanwhile, kept saying: "It's nothing. A few gifts."

It was only then that the story related to us by Saad Eddin Wahba at his home in Cairo fell into place, and I could understand Mansi's suspicious behaviour at the airport, running from place to place, whispering and mumbling.

The contents were replaced in the boxes and the covers put back on. The officer remained silent for a while, as if he had lost the ability to think and speak. And although he must have witnessed scores of unusual incidents in the course of his work, he looked as if he had never seen such a thing before. Finally, he raised his head. Turning to the Qataris, he said, in such a quiet voice that it was difficult to identify whether it concealed anger or astonishment: "This gentleman is working with you?"

I was hoping they would say no, but one of them hastily said: "Yes."

As we went out of the airport, I said to Mansi: "Listen, from this point on, we should part ways. I swear to God, you are not accompanying me. We are not staying in the same hotel. You don't know me. I don't know you."

22

The Qataris booked me into the Holiday Inn, the newly built hotel that was later to be gutted by the war, as were all the big hotels in that part of the world: the Phoenicia, the Alcazar, the St Georges. Beirut at the time was in the midst of a construction boom; you could be away for a month or so and when you returned you would see new hotels and buildings that had not been there before. It was as though some children demolished, in a moment of frustration, the sand palaces they had spent hours building on the beach.

I know that area between Zaitounay Bay and Ain El Mraisseh very well. During my time at the BBC, I would be dispatched to their Beirut office in the Nazlat al-Daouk building in Phoenicia Street, which wound down to the sea by St Georges Hotel. Hassan El Milleigi, the 'king' of Ain El Mraisseh, and the late Mahmoud Naseer, the 'king' of Zaitounay, were Egyptians who had migrated to Beirut and made a permanent domicile there. They produced pro-grammes for the BBC, and were very famous at the time, particularly Hassan El Milleigi, whose life was a legend more thrilling than Mansi's. I came to know Beirut through them and through Salah Ahmed, who was the press attaché at the Sudanese Embassy.

I had stayed with Salah upon coming to Beirut for the first time, in 1958, on the 12th floor of Mangaara Building on the outskirts of Hamra. I remember that morning very well. I looked out at a city swinging between the mountain and the sea; the morning light was dazzling, in sharp contrast to London's shy sun and cloudy sky. The blueness of the sea mixed with the blueness of the sky and the reflection of sunrays from the roofs of houses and buildings and with the greenery on the foothills – it was as though one were looking at a fictitious city. The Gulf of Jounieh was a stone's throw away. And that must be the top of Baskinta where Mikhail Naimy once lived in seclusion. I visited him there later.

With a little extra effort, perhaps one could have seen as far as Cyprus. Here, you are at a crossroads and a meeting point of civilisations; what were once the lands of Lydia and the Levant. To the west was 'Europa', and to the south were 'Africa Proconsularis' and Nile Valley Africa. To the east were 'Arabia Petrea' and 'Arabia Deserta', and the lands of the Qahtanis and the Adnanis – and beyond that stood Mesopotamia, the land of Babylon and Assyria. Then came Christianity followed by Islam – one building on the other.

At noon, Mansi appeared, cheerful and smiling as if nothing had happened. In fact my anger had subsided by then and Mansi's ordeal at the airport seemed trivial compared to the impending evil that loomed high. I had seen the first signs last night as I entered the hotel.

Scores of armed youngsters glared at people coming in and out of the hotel. Then Ahmed Saeed Mohammadiyeh, the owner of publisher Dar al-'Awda, came in and confirmed that the country was heading towards a terrible explosion.

Mansi was clearly oblivious to all this. "You know what," he said, "I'm staying at a nice hotel on al-Hamra Street. Its owners are lovely Armenian chaps; they gave me an entire suite at a price lower than what you're paying for a single room here. Why did you choose to stay in this rubbish place?"

"You have friends here in Beirut?"

"Oooh! So very many. These chaps are old friends. I always stay with them – they are hilarious!"

Then he added: "By the way, what's wrong with you? Why the angry face? You missed a lovely night."

Mansi pronounced the 'g' sound unlike most Egyptians: for the word in Egyptian dialect that meant 'very', literally 'strong' in English, he would say '*gawi*' as was the practice in Upper Egypt, rather than '*awee*' as prevalent elsewhere in Egypt.

"Let's go – let's not waste any more time. I've booked you a suite like mine. You'll love the hotel. You will enjoy the company of these lovely chaps. We'll have fun!"

I told him I had decided to leave that same day because the city was tense and I sensed danger.

"Come on! Stop this nonsense. Everything is just fine.

Nothing's going to happen. Stay with us there three more days."

Then I asked him about the boxes.

"I sold them," he said.

"Sold them? I thought you said they were gifts."

"Did you believe that? Who would I give lingerie to?"

"Damn you! The Qatari Embassy staff will think I am your partner in a smuggling business."

He was thrilled at discovering that he had put me in such a predicament.

"These are the same boxes Saad Eddin was referring to, aren't they?"

"Yeah. All my attempts to get them through to Kuwait failed."

"So you took them back to Cairo."

"And I left them at the airport for a full year. And when I found out that you were going to Beirut – a senior employee of the State of Qatar on an official visit – it was a golden opportunity that I didn't want to miss."

"And so you presented yourself as a Qatari government employee and a member of an official delegation."

"My respected friend," he said, laughing in his weird way that always indicated he had successfully cheated someone. "You don't seem to have noticed. I had the consignment shipped from Cairo to Beirut in your name!"

"What do you mean in my name?"

"It means that I made all the officers at Cairo Airport believe that the consignment belonged to you. Why do you think I kept running back and forth that day?"

Despite everything, I found myself bursting into a fit of laughter.

"But how come they are all ladies' garments – in fact just lingerie? Damn you! You must have cheated someone!"

"I will tell you the story. A Jewish merchant in Washington had gone bankrupt and had to put his stock in a clearance sale. I bought the whole lot for peanuts, but I couldn't get it through to Egypt, Kuwait or Beirut. The customs duties there were higher than the original price. When I found you I thought to myself: 'Problem solved'."

"Did you make a good profit?

"They were thrilled to take it – those amazing chaps. They bought it all for a decent price. You know they were high end brands: silk, great stuff."

"Were you not claiming that you were a rich man, owner of a language school, a restaurant, a tourist company and a house in the best part of Washington?"

"You know who my next door neighbour is there? Robert Kennedy. My kids play with his children every day."

"But since you are such a big shot and your kids are friends of Robert Kennedy's, how can you not feel ashamed for behaving like a beggar?"

Another prolonged fit of laughter. That was the ultimate objective: doing something strange and daring that had no justification or meaning except that it was going to be another episode in his myth-rich life.

I left Mansi behind in Beirut, quite confident that he was going to manage his affairs one way or another. As the Middle East Airlines plane ascended, the sky was pleasantly clear and the sea looked like an endless fanciful dream, and that wonderful city, with all its precious, beautiful and noble treasures, stood there, the roofs of its houses glittering under the Mediterranean sun, in anticipation of the impending earthquake.

23

I left Mansi behind in Beirut on that day in 1975 that marked the eruption of civil war in Lebanon. In a sense, his presence there on that particular day was not totally irrelevant: wasn't his own life a series of 'absurd' improvised acts that hardly had any meaning or justification? But they would always come to pleasant conclusions and would not last too long. Unlike this war – what was the point behind it? It had taken too long and brought about a cocktail of calamities. Just as Zuhayr had eloquently described it:

War is nothing else but what you have known and yourselves tasted,

It's not a tale told at random, a vague conjecture;

When you stir it up, it's a hateful thing you have stirred; ravenous it is, once you whet its appetite; it bursts aflame,

Then it grinds you as a millstone grinds on its cushion.

Yearly it conceives, birth upon birth, and with twins for issue –

Very ill-omened are the boys it bears you, every one of them the like of Ahmar of Ad; then it gives suck, and weans them.

Look, for God's sake. Weren't these verses and the remaining lines of this poem, created some 13 centuries ago, the most accurate and lively description of war ever made up to this date?

Of course one cannot help but admire the genius of this poet who had composed verses that have remained relevant for all this long period of time. Yet one cannot help but feel sad that history has not taken a prudent course since the days of Abs and Dubyan[6], despite all the ensuing events, and despite all the ideas produced and the blood and tears shed.

Why should one think that the Lebanese are the only war igniters? In the Sudan, we have been embroiled in a war for over 30 years now; a war that has devastated the country's natural resources and claimed countless lives. No one knows how it erupted or when it will come to an end. Besides, it was no less heinous than the Lebanese war — and if the Lebanese war has given birth to ill-omened offspring, as Zuhayr said, ours was no less productive. But now I am talking about Beirut, which I hold in the same high regard as I do Khartoum, and my grief at Sudan's tragedies is no deeper than my grief at Lebanon's.

That was only natural. I had known the Lebanese during the good days and found them sincere, openhanded and faithful. During the wretched years, they stood fast with unwavering patience; their hospitals kept receiving the victims under a ceaseless showering of bombs. Their planes continued to roam the skies and would resume their dives

6 Two pre-Islamic Arabian tribes that were at war for almost 40 years.

in and out of the airport as soon as it was reopened to traffic. Their newspapers continued to come out perfectly on time. Their bookshops were overflowing with books; their printing presses continued to run full swing as did their factories. Once the guns came to a halt, shops would open and people would take to the streets, making their way through the wreckage of buildings, fighting the forces of evil and death with their natural disposition towards peace. These are the 'ordinary' Lebanese who constitute the majority. While the war has dealt them horrendous calamities, it has also rekindled in them the spirit of sympathy, sacrifice, and noble acts. Were it not for those 'ordinary' people, the leaders would not have found anything left worth fighting for. The same applies to the Sudan: had it not been for the kindness, humaneness, and wisdom of the ordinary people, Sudan would have been torn apart like a ragged dress, and the leaders' follies would have irretrievably destroyed whatever remained of it.

Like the ancient poets, each one attracted to a particular mark or vestige, I was keen to visit Beirut every year or every two or three years, even during the war years. On each visit I would find that something had been destroyed: a restaurant I used to frequent; a café where I sat with friends; or a hotel I once stayed in.

This neighbourhood, laden with all these memories, had been burnt down:

– the BBC office, once a meeting-place for men of letters, poets, journalists, academics, religious men and politicians;

– the house of Hassan El Milleigi, once a popular club and gathering place for us;

– the balcony of Mahmoud Naseer (the 'king' of Zaitounay), where we frequently sat and looked out on the city and the sea and watched the planes land and take off;

– Dar Shi'r (House of Poetry) on the other side of Phoenicia Street opposite to the BBC office. Whenever I felt a need for a break from work, I would go down to Yusuf al-Khal and spend an hour or two with him. He was a wonderful person whom you might disagree with but would never fail to love. Far from bigotry and dogmatism, his controversial ideas were rather a product of a fervent soul and an unquenchable passion for innovation.

It was in Beirut that my first work had been published and it was in Beirut that I had first come to be known. And although I eventually came to know other mountains, seas, and cities that were bigger and worlds that were more expansive, I remain attached to this city as if we had time-honoured ties from ancient times. I was by no means alone in this, however. It is a city that lives in the hearts of many. Ghada al-Samman, the Khansa of our time, wrote moving elegies, as did Buland al-Haydari, Nizar Qabbani, Sameer Attallah, Muhammad al-Faytury, Adonis, Mahmoud Darwish, and others. And Khalida Said wrote wonderful articles in *Al-Majalla* magazine. Surely, 'love' will rebuild what has been destroyed by ill-will and spite. For all this love cannot simply be in vain.

And perhaps that faint glimpse is a prelude to daylight. God has deployed a group of distinguished men of resolve and a high sense of honour who remind us of Al-Harith ibn Awf and Haram ibn Sinan, the two great men who had taken upon themselves to pay blood money, cure the injured, and wipe away the tears of bereaved women and orphans. And perhaps this holy spot has showered its blessings on the conferees in Taif, making them more responsive to the heartfelt appeals and to reason. Hopefully a genius poet like Zuhayr would emerge to give this war the censure it deserves and accord those great people the praise they are worthy of. Who said eulogies are unbecoming? Great deeds always deserve to be documented in great poetry. As the great poet al-Mutanabbi put it:

The creator of glory and the composer of exquisite verses are equal in merit,

For both are masters of subtle concepts and profound meanings.

24

I arrived in Sydney at night. From the air, it looked no different than most cities: streams of light of varying width and length, one on a hillside, another in a valley, a riverbank or a seashore. At night, those cities look as if they are hanging midway between the sky and the earth, between darkness and darkness. It is so depressing that man – this strong and weak, rich and poor, creature – should keep trying desperately to prove himself in such a gloomy environment – an alien universe. That feeling must have besieged our great poet–philosopher Abu al-'Ala' Al-Ma'arri:

> *In the heart of the night a wolf once howled,*
> *Perchance another howler will return the cry.*
> *But no wolves were around, none heard the call*
> *A fruitless attempt it was, an idle try!*
> *Behold the noble steeds huddled at the gates of a mighty sire,*
> *Yet dreary are his days, foreboding, dire.*[7]

---

7 Verse translated by Dr Mahmoud Abbas Masoud

Here is an expansive swathe of light on a sea shore. I left Doha in the middle of summer, forgetting that Doha's summer meant that it was winter in Sydney – but who would remember winter while in the throes of a scorching summer? So I came to Sydney ill-prepared for its bitter cold.

Also a feeling of alienation pervaded my soul, even though I was a veteran traveller who had a passion for roaming the world. Perhaps this time I felt I had travelled too far from my familiar world. Oh, how distant these localities are from Wadi Hawar, Wadi al-Khozama, and Wadi al-Aqeeq!

And I had no acquaintances here, so no one was there to receive me at the airport. Fortunately, though, the passport officer gave me an entry pass in less than a minute. He did not seem to have flipped through the passport pages or checked if I had a visa. No, a glance at the passport, a glance at me – and he wished me a pleasant stay. I was taken by surprise, given what had happened at their embassy in Delhi; had it not been for Mansi, I would not have come here in the first place.

I did not have a hotel booking. So I thought I should go to the Hilton. This chain of hotels that Mr Hilton had built to commemorate his contribution to human civilisation gives you the same hotel wherever you go. The rates are more or less the same, and so is the room size. Indeed, you can enter any room blindly without any difficulty finding your way to the bathroom, the closet, or the bed. A typical American, Mr Hilton seems to have wanted to accomplish the maximum benefit of this worldly life as well as the hereafter; for there is a copy of the Bible in each room of his hotels in all parts of the world. By that he was hoping to make millions in this earthly world as well as bountiful divine rewards in the hereafter. Thank God that nowadays one can see in hotel rooms, in some Muslim countries, a copy of the Holy Qur'an and an arrow pointing to Mecca to where prayers would be directed.

The receptionist asked if I had a booking. I absentmindedly said "Yes". To my surprise, he did find a booking in my name.

"Yes. There is a booking in your name. You work for the World Tourist Company – don't you?"

My God! So Mansi must be in town.

I had had enough of him. It is not uncommon for one to feel fed up with someone that they love. He had wanted to come to Sydney via Bombay while I had insisted on taking a shorter route through Bangkok. So we had parted, each one taking the route of his choice. I was hoping he would go astray to any other destination so that I could devote myself to the mission that the State of Qatar had sent me on, away from Mansi's mischief. Now, however, I am happy to know that he is in Sydney; that I have a friend in this strange city, in this distant world. As it turned out later, his presence was a blessing and he was to prove a great help to me. However, I did not like to be referred to as an employee of Mansi's World Tourist Company.

"Actually, I work for the Government of Qatar, not the World Tourist Company."

"Ah," was the receptionist's reply, and only later did I

come to understand why he said "Ah" in that strange tone.

Mansi visited me just after midday, after I had had a long sleep. Despite everything, Mansi was too polite and considerate to bother others – except occasionally – and would leave once he felt they wanted to be left alone.

As I opened the door, he blurted out without saying hello – as if we had not parted in Delhi: "Why do you insist on acting in this stupid way?"

"What?"

"Saying you are a Government of Qatar employee – I had told them you worked for our company."

"Isn't it the truth?"

"You know how much you lost because of your stupidity? Fifty per cent; as a tourist company, we are entitled to 50% discount in hotels."

"But I am here on an official assignment. Do you want me to come to this remote part of the world and lie for the sake of saving a few dollars? Not only that, but also to claim that I work for an obscure tourist company like yours?"

"OK, sir. You will always remain the idiot you are, claiming you never lie and all this rubbish. Wait a minute! Now I understand! You must have a lot of money. I forgot you work for the oil-rich guys."

Unfortunately, as I later discovered, Mansi was truly convinced that I had a lot of money because I worked for an oil-rich country. He played host to scores of people at the hotel, always charging the bills to my room account. These trivial games were a great source of joy to him. During our earlier days back in London, he would go to the BBC cafeteria, take whatever food he wanted and sit himself down comfortably without bothering to pay. He would not do that furtively, but rather boldly as if he were exercising an undisputed right. When he returned from the US to live on his estate in the south of England, I visited him with my family for a weekend. He was hospitable as usual and when he drove us back to the railway station, I noticed that he was jesting with the guard. Suddenly, he sneaked in without buying an platform ticket, which was no more than a few shillings.

I said to him: "Damn you. No matter how rich you become, you remain the beggar you are."

He laughed at my comment, for these acts were merely driven by a childish desire for fun.

Now, at the Sydney Hilton, I asked him: "How did you know my arrival time?"

He laughed, for a reason you will learn later, and said: "It was my friend Dorga who gave me your flight details."

"But how could you be certain that I was going to come to this particular hotel?"

"Telepathy. I was sure you were going to come here. Didn't you know I could foretell the future? But even if you had gone to a different hotel, I would have found you. You couldn't have escaped me."

25

One Friday afternoon, Mansi called me from London; I had not heard from him for months.

"Listen, Tayeb. I will stop over in Doha tomorrow on my way to Riyadh and spend a couple of days with you."

"Tomorrow I won't be in Doha. I will be travelling."

"Where to?"

"Delhi."

"What have you got there?"

"Business trip."

"Really? OK. Listen. It's a good idea. I will come with you. How do you feel about that? I haven't been to India before."

"This is not a trip from London to Oxford or Edinburgh. I am telling you that I am going to Delhi, then to Sydney, and on to Tokyo. And it's an official visit – business – I am not going for leisure."

"So what? It will be a great trip. You do your work and we can also have fun and explore. Now stop fussing. I have made up my mind. Just give me the flight details."

"I am leaving at 7am. Now it's 4pm. You hardly have time to make a booking."

"7am? Ah – the BA flight. I was going to book on Gulf Air. No problem. Did you forget I have a tourist company? OK. See you tomorrow at the airport. It's going to be a great trip."

Mansi would occasionally stop over in Doha on his frequent trips to and from Riyadh where he had a business, a wife and a house. I once received him at Doha Airport. It was the first time that I saw him in a traditional Arab dress: *abaya, thobe, ghutrah* and *agal*[8], and a tiny, triangular beard – no moustache. He looked like a westerner performing the role of an Arab in an American film. I found out that he was being held at the passport desk, and went down there and asked the passport officer about him.

He told me: "This man holds an American passport; his name is Michael something. He looks like an Arab, he speaks Arabic, and he says he is a Muslim. What's this? He must be a spy."

Mansi kept laughing; clearly amused by the perplexing situation that he had created.

"He is not a spy," I said to the Qatari young man. "He is even worse. But please allow him to enter and I will take full responsibility for him."

Fortunately, Mansi's laughter – which in itself was adequate proof that he could not possibly conceal a secret or

---

8 *Abaya* is a cloak; *thobe* is an ankle-length garment; *ghutrah* is a traditional head-dress, and *agal* is a black cord used to keep the *ghutrah* in place on the wearer's head

harbour any evil – was contagious. The Qatari chap could not help but burst out laughing. Finally, he let him in, but held his passport as a precautionary measure.

I hung up, wondering how he could possibly make it in time. At 7 am, once I boarded the plane, I saw my friend in flesh and blood. Looking brisk and fresh, he must have slept throughout the flight from London. Napoleon was said to have had that talent of sleeping at any time, anywhere, sometimes for a few minutes, and would still wake up fresh and energetic as if he had slept for hours. If genius were measured by how quickly one can fall asleep, then I would bear witness that Mansi was a true genius. He once slept in the courtyard of the Great Mosque in Mecca between the Maghrib and Isha prayers, oblivious to the hustle and bustle of worshippers around him.

That was during my first Umrah, and he was in my company along with a young man from the Saudi National Guard. We would be on the fifth round of our Sai ritual walk between the symbolic hills of Safa and Marwa, while Mansi would be lagging behind on the second round. More than once, spotting him running in the wrong direction, we had to rush over to him and redirect him to the right path, but he would soon go astray again. When he finally completed the ritual, he fell into a deep sleep, as if he were in his bedroom, until we woke him up when it was time to return to Jeddah.

"Is this a place for sleeping, useless?"

He said: "I can fall asleep at any time. Why not? I am sin-free."

He was thrilled to see the astonishment on my face as I took the seat next to him that he had booked for me. Rather than standing up to greet me, he kept stroking his belly and looking around as if he wanted to show off his new miracle to some invisible audience.

He never stopped talking all the way to Delhi, depriving me of the pleasure of looking down at new cities from the air in daytime, when one can have a bird's eye view of the city and see its mountains, desert, rivers, or other features. Perhaps that is the image that always remains imprinted in the memory after one forgets such details as street names, architecture, traffic, etc.

In India, Dr Hassan Ni'mah, Qatar's Ambassador, and Ibrahim Taha Ayoub, Sudan's Ambassador, both took to Mansi so fast that they looked as though they were old friends. So Mansi loved the place and really enjoyed his time to the full. Despite his intelligence and diverse experience, Mansi, may God rest his soul in peace, never lost his child-like innocence. He would be at his best when he felt he was welcome and liked. That would clear his soul, freshen up his mind, and unleash his quirky sense of humour.

Even Dorga, an Indian employee of the Qatari Embassy whom the Ambassador had tasked with arranging my meetings and facilitating my movements, was so fascinated by Mansi that he devoted himself entirely to him.

26

Dr Hassan Ni'mah, Qatar's Ambassador to Delhi, is a truly unique person – one of a kind. He has a PhD in Arabic language from Cambridge, and has been in his Delhi post for over ten years now. He has developed a strong passion for India, its arts and heritage, and has grown so emotionally attached to it that he does not want to leave for any other post. Whenever he felt a transfer was imminent, he would rush to Doha and ask the authorities to leave him where he was. They always responded positively. That was one good thing about Qatar: if they felt an ambassador was happy where he was they would not transfer him. Thanks to their foresight, our friend Abdulla al-Jida remained in his Rabat station for a full decade.

Through his strong association with the Sudanese in Cambridge and in Doha, Hassan Ni'mah memorised the poetry of al-Hardallo[9] and Tijani Yusuf Bashir.[10] Whenever

---

9   A famous Sudanese Bedouin poet
10 A prominent Sudanese poet

he met a Sudanese, he would greet him with a famous Sudanese expression: "*Ya zool!*[11] I am reposing and relaxed; singing praise for al-Mustapha[12]", which meant that life has been particularly kind to him and he is so thankful that he wants to chant praises for Prophet Mohammed, may the blessings of God be on him.

That was the mood he was in when Mansi and I met him in Delhi. He lived in a beautiful, spacious house, a combination of Islamic and Mongol architecture embellished with shades of the 'British Raj' style. It had an open, green courtyard, which he used as a grazing space for his cows that provided him with fresh milk. He led a very simple life, depending primarily on yogurt for his sustenance. A frequent traveller, he toured the east and west of India, and studied its music, arts, architecture and fine art. He was an eloquent poet and narrator of Arabic poetry, both classical and modern. He had a strong liking for the metaphysical Muslim poets like Jalal al-Din Rumi, Ibn al-Farid, al-Shirazi and Saadi. Thus, it was not difficult for him to find a place for Mansi in these spacious worlds; and they took to each other effortlessly.

Another person who liked Mansi was Sudan's Ambassador Ibrahim Taha Ayoub, who was from Wadi Halfa in the north. People from that area are regarded by historians as the earliest settlers in the Nile Valley; their settlement extended from southern Egypt all the way to North Sudan,

---

11 A common nickname for a Sudanese
12 A nickname for Prophet Mohammed

creating a strong bond of integration between the two nations. Their land was submerged under the waters of the High Dam; the residents on the Egyptian side were relocated to the northern edges of Upper Egypt, while those on the Sudanese side were moved to the Butana plains in eastern Sudan.

Now in hindsight, I wonder which option would have been better pursued: maintaining that bond or trading it for more water and electricity for Egypt? Only God knows.

The Halfawis are renowned for honesty, personal integrity, and mockery. Furthermore, they are very sharp-minded and highly skilled. Their ancestors had retained the custodianship of Pharaonic temples and they had inherent loyalty to the 'Establishment' running in their blood. When the Arabs introduced Islam to them they embraced it willingly because they felt it was a true faith. One of their ancestors was probably Bilal, the Prophet's caller to prayers. More recently, other prominent Halfawis included Jamal Mohammed Ahmed, a former ambassador and Minister of Foreign Affairs and one of the most notable thinkers in the Nile Valley, who was not accorded the recognition he deserved. Another eminent figure from Wadi Halfa was Daoud Abdel Lateef, a governor and minister renowned for his shrewdness and good sense of humour; and Muhammad Nur al-Din, one of the founders of the National Unionist Party and an ardent advocate of unification with Egypt.

It was reported that Muhammad Nur al-Din was an intimate friend of Abdallah Khalil, although they stood at variance politically. Khalil was an Umma Party leader who later became prime minister in the first cabinet set up by his party. Both Nur al-Din and Khalil led an austere life and upon learning that they were both in financial trouble, Abd al-Rahman al-Mahdi, the leader of the Ansar sect, sent an aide to each one with some financial help. The messenger went first to Abdallah Khalil. When he handed him the money, Khalil said: "Take it to Mohammed Nur al-Din: he needs it more desperately than I do." The messenger told him that there was a separate parcel for Nur al-Din.

When the messenger went to Muhammad Nur al-Din and handed him the parcel, he said: "Take it to Abdallah Khalil. He needs it more badly than I do." When the messenger went back to al-Mahdi and told him what had happened, tears welled up in al-Mahdi's eyes.

A couple of years ago, while in Amman I incidentally came across Ahmed al-Mahdi, son of Abd al-Rahman al-Mahdi, and uncle of Sadiq al-Mahdi. We had met earlier in London when he had been studying at Oxford and I later worked under him briefly in 1966 when he was the Information Minister in Sadiq al-Mahdi's first cabinet. I asked him about that story and he confirmed it was true. He then said: "I will tell you another one which is even more amazing."

"A delegation of the Soviet Communist Party arrived in Sudan at the invitation of the Sudanese Communist Party. Abd al-Rahman al-Mahdi summoned Abdel Khaliq Mahjub, Secretary General of the Sudanese Communist Party, whom he treated as his own son, as he was a friend of his father's. He said to Abdel Khaliq: 'I understand you have guests from the Soviet Union. I know your party can't afford to provide our guests with the hospitality they deserve. We are all keen that they should have a good impression about the Sudan and about the hospitality of their Sudanese counterparts. So what are you going to do for them?

"'Well,' said Abdel Khaliq, 'we haven't decided yet. We will do what we can afford to do – Perhaps a tea party.'

"'No,' said al-Mahdi. 'A tea party is not enough. Bring them here for dinner. I will host a grand dinner party for them.'"

And so it happened that communists, both Sudanese and Bolsheviks, dined at the table of Abd al-Rahman al-Mahdi, the religious man and Imam of the Ansar sect and patron of the Umma Party."

These are shining examples of earlier generations, may God rest their souls in peace.

Another prominent figure who belonged to the Halfawi tribe, the people of Ibrahim Taha Ayoub, was Muhammad Tawfiq, one of the pillars of the Democratic Unionist Party who served as foreign minister in Sadiq al-Mahdi's cabinet that followed the glorious Rajab Uprising. Now he is in jail! Another one of Sudan's wonders: at any given time, there are always leaders at the helm while their opponents are behind bars – as if that expansive land is too small to accommodate them all. One of my direst wishes before leaving this world – now that my time is shrinking like a forenoon shadow, and the horizon that once seemed too distant is fast approaching – is to see all people free and unrestrained, and that prisons play host exclusively to their true clientele: murderers and criminals.

Ibrahim Taha Ayoub was smart, so he was attracted to that quality in Mansi. And he was good-humoured so he liked Mansi's cheerfulness. And he was witty, so he found one who was peerless.

We were guests of Dr Hassan Ni'mah in Delhi in the summer of 1980, a night engulfed in silence except for the sound of an Indian sitar being played in the distance sending out heart-breaking melodies. The heart, at the time, was carefree, immune to the agonies of separation, and beyond the reach of that spectre that once gave the great Arab poet, al-Buhturi, sleepless nights:

> *Haven't you seen the flashes of lightning leap,*
> *And the departing spectre of the penurious maid?*
> *A wraith-like phantom from Sawa came to her at night,*
> *While at Batn Marr we're sound asleep.*

27

In Delhi, I discovered another quality in Mansi that I hadn't noticed before. He shared with some animals the ability to adapt their bodies to their habitat – turning green when they lived in a green environment and brown when in a sandy environment. But he was by no means moody. Far from it, he was always truly himself. In India, he seemed to have acquired an Indian physique. His body colour became darker – or so I thought – and his hair – or, more accurately, whatever was left of it, looked very much like an Indian's. Even his facial expressions and hand movements seemed to be similar to those made by Indians. Although he only learned a few sentences in Hindi, the way he pronounced them gave the impression that he had an excellent command of that language. One should add to this his amazing talent in eliminating distances with others and his natural empathy with the poor and needy. No wonder, then, that Dorga warmed to him instantly and devoted himself entirely to him.

In many instances, I had to take a taxi to a meeting with a state official because I could not find Dorga on time to give me a lift.

"Where have you been, Dorga?" I would ask later. "I was with Dr Ahmed," would be his answer.

Occasionally, I had to take Mansi along to my meetings only because I found out it was the only way of guaranteeing that Dorga would be available to give me the pleasure of his company.

Were the Qataris to know that Mansi was to be involved in this mission in any way, they would have called it off and assigned it to someone else. Qatar had taken seriously the resolutions of the Arab Information Ministers' conferences, particularly with respect to the negative image of Arabs in the world. It took upon itself the task of examining the viability of creating a mega media foundation after the pattern of such world-renowned institutions as the Ford and Rockefeller Foundations, the British Council, Goethe Institutes, and similar cultural and media bodies in France, Sweden and Japan. This pan-Arab foundation was to be created with huge funding from oil-rich states, and was to be active in the arenas of information, culture, thought and art, promoting the Arabs' rich heritage to all parts of the world. In other words, it would seek to foster a proactive cultural role for Arabs in the international arena. Imagine if this wonderful dream were to come true! The foundation was envisaged as enjoying full autonomy and having a free hand in probing all means to achieve its ultimate objective. I should mention here, in all fairness, that His Highness the Emir of

Qatar had shown immense enthusiasm and unequivocal support for this idea.

So Qatar selected Mahmoud Al Sharif, the prominent media figure who had served as Director of Qatar's Information Ministry before me, to go on a mission to the USA, and sent me on a tour of India, Australia, Japan, and some West European countries. Our mission was to examine the image of Arabs prevalent in these countries and evaluate the indigenous models of the institution under study. We were highly impressed by what we saw. Unfortunately, that great dream was nipped in the bud.

On the personal level, though, I must say I benefitted immensely, thanks to the State of Qatar, without whose generous gesture I could not possibly have visited those distant countries and alien worlds.

We arrived in Delhi on the same day that Sanjay Gandhi, the eldest son of the Prime Minister, died in a plane crash. Mrs Gandhi had been grooming him to be her successor. He was an adventurous young man who was profoundly loved by many and bitterly hated by many others. Now that he was dead, we found out that most Indians – save for a few – were profoundly grieved by his loss. Dr Hassan Ni'mah, for one, was very sad; he had been a close friend of Sanjay's, and had been counting on him to support Arab causes.

India was not entirely new to me. I had read the poetry of Rabindranath Tagore and the biographies of Gandhi and Nehru. I had watched the films of the gifted director Satyajit Ray and had developed a strong passion for Ravi

Shankar's music. I was not far from Nehru as he delivered his country's address in New York in 1960. As high school students in Sudan in the late 1940s, we were fascinated by the ideas of Mahatma Gandhi and followed with keen interest India's struggle against the British colonial powers. In fact, the creation of the Graduates' General Congress in Sudan to spearhead the struggle for independence was largely inspired by the Indian Congress Movement. We knew India's leaders by name and were familiar with its geography and history and fascinated by the names of its cities. We still memorise Shawqi's poem in praise of Gandhi when Gandhi was on his way to attend the Round Table Conference in London:

> *Greetings from the Nile, O Gandhi,*
> *And a flower bouquet from me,*
> *Greetings from the milkmaid of sheep*
> *Greetings from the gown weaver.*

We were particularly moved by this line:
> *And say: call in your snakes:*
> *The charmer has come from India!*

We felt that that skinny man, naked save for a cotton wrap he had woven himself, embodied a profound meaning, which had ignited our imagination; it was a meaning which we had read about in the biographies of early Muslim leaders but were yet to see in real life, except in very rare cases.

Sudan and India, both being former British colonies, had many things in common: systems of government, administration, education, and city planning. Britons who had worked in India were occasionally seconded to us. Of those, I remember an army officer, a Colonel Exeter, who came to teach us English. He chose to teach us a book that we could not appreciate at that early age: *Memoirs of a Fox-Hunting Man* by Siegfried Sassoon. Only years later did we realise that it was one of the classics of English literature. Back in those days, however, we did not like the book and asked our colonel teacher to replace it. He flamed up with rage and scolded us in an overly arrogant tone that angered us. When he came the next day, he found all the copies of the book stacked on his desk.

"What is the meaning of this?"

No one answered. We kept looking at him, silently. He spared no swear word, calling us uneducable savages, before storming out of the classroom. When that came to the attention of the principal, a kindhearted Scottish man who loved Sudan and understood the characteristics of its people, he came to our rescue and within a week had sent the colonel back home.

To us, that was our first act of peaceful resistance, undertaken while we were still under twenty years old. That act was not inspired by the philosophy of Mahatma Gandhi, though. It was part of our natural disposition to resist arrogance and hegemony with silent contempt, but when things went beyond the limit we would abruptly rise up as violently as the flooding of the Nile and the rage of storms in the Atmur desert. We had done that with the Turks, with the British, and with indigenous rulers.

"Halt, friends, this is Azza's dwelling" – quoting the ancient Arab poet. Here is Delhi, capital of all India, and the pearl of the British Empire during its glorious times. It reminds one of the colonial rule in Khartoum – but they are different in many respects.

Very much like al-Shahrazawri's friend, who "was following the trail of his friend", my friend Mansi was on my trail, while his friend Dorga was on his trail. All of us were making our way towards a horizon that looked both within and beyond reach.

28

As Australia had no embassy in Doha at the time – they still do not, to the best of my knowledge – I had planned to get an entry visa in Delhi. We called the Australian Consul in Bahrain who promised to write to their embassy in Delhi to issue us a visa.

We went to the Embassy: Mansi carrying his American passport, while I had my Sudanese passport that I had clung to all those years and adamantly refused to trade in for any other one despite the troubles it had caused me. Even in Sudan, I faced considerable difficulty, both entering and leaving the country. Our passport is valid for only two years when every other nation in the world issues its citizens passports that are valid for five or even ten years. Besides, we are required to obtain something called an exit visa, as if we were in East Germany – even there, the walls have collapsed and people are now free to go in and out. I entered the Consul's office before Mansi. I had already filled in the forms and completed all the formalities.

The Consul flicked through the passport pages, patiently

screening it as if he had never seen anything like it before. Finally, he said: "I am very sorry, Mr Salih. We haven't yet received the approval from Canberra. You will need to wait – perhaps it will come in a week's time."

"I am afraid I don't have time. I have to leave tomorrow or the day after."

"I'm sorry about that."

"But why Canberra? I know you are authorised to issue visas without having to refer to Canberra."

"There are cases when we have to get the Ministry's approval. This is standard procedure. All countries do this. Anyway, no problem. We will contact Canberra. You can collect your visa from our embassy in Singapore."

"But I'm not going to Singapore."

"It's on your way. Why don't you stop over for a day or two?"

"Listen. If getting permission to enter your country is so difficult, I will cancel my trip altogether. You know that I am going to Australia on an official assignment, not for leisure. But thanks anyway."

I stormed out of the Consul's office, ignoring Mansi who tried in vain to talk to me, and went straight back to the hotel.

Hardly an hour had passed when my room telephone rang.

"Mr Salih?"

"Yes."

"I'm calling from the Australian Embassy. I am the Ambassador's secretary. He would like to talk to you."

A cheerful voice came to my ears: "Mr. Salih . . . I am terribly sorry for the misunderstanding with the Consul. He did not know you. Dr Michael is now sitting with me. He has explained everything to me. I would be delighted, Mr Salih, if you would kindly come to my office – now, if that suits you. You will find the visa ready. Do you have a means of transport? We can send you a car."

Of course, I did not have a means of transport – the car and Dorga were both for Mansi's exclusive service, as usual. Yet, I did not want to exploit the Ambassador's kindness so I took a taxi. On the way, I was able to guess what had happened: Mansi quickly realises what had happened during my meeting with the Consul. He storms into the Ambassador's office – without permission as usual. In a few minutes, they are chatting like old friends. He draws up an exaggerated picture of his importance first, then my importance, and thirdly of the importance of our 'joint' mission in Australia.

They welcomed me at the door and led me ceremoniously to the Ambassador's office where I saw my friend Mansi, or Dr Michael, sitting relaxed, drinking tea. The Ambassador rose to his feet and came forward to welcome me. He was in his early forties, as tall and energetic as you would expect an Australian to be – a blend of a Harvard and a Cambridge graduate.

I could see that Mansi and the Ambassador were now on familiar terms. The Australians, like the Americans, are naturally simple and down to earth. In an attempt to show me how much he had achieved, Mansi said:

"Did you know that Richard has a PhD in Political Science from Yale?"

"Richard?" I asked, pretending ignorance.

"His Excellency the Ambassador."

The Ambassador said: "I am very sorry for what happened, Mr Salih. You know consuls go by the book. We can't blame them, of course. I understand from Dr Michael that you are a prominent writer and a famous figure in Qatar."

Mansi was certain that I was going to disown all these titles he had bestowed upon me. So before I could reply, he said: "Mr Salih is a very modest person; no wonder the Consul didn't accord him the treatment he deserved."

We talked about the Australian writer Patrick White and the Australian painter Sidney Nolan and the opera singer Joan Sutherland. Because of the long distance between Australia and the centres of civilisation and being aware that Europeans in particular considered them to be savage and unrefined, the Australians are particularly keen to present themselves as civilised people with a strong passion for thought and culture. So they are proud of their compatriots who gain worldwide repute. That was why the Ambassador was happy to note that we were fairly knowledgeable about Australia.

He was a truly nice person and we enjoyed his company, and it was obvious that he was prepared to keep us for as long as he possibly could. He gave me my passport back, duly stamped with a gratis entry visa. And he must have even pulled a few strings with the authorities at home; for the passports officer at Sydney Airport, as I mentioned earlier, issued me an entry pass without caring to examine my passport.

"I would love to invite you to dinner tonight if you don't have any other plans."

I had absolutely no doubt that Mansi would have accepted without hesitation – that would have been a new affiliation opening up before him; a new experience that he would not hesitate to throw himself into as zealously as poets and artists would do. I too do that sometimes.

I quickly apologised to the Ambassador and I must have sounded resolute because Mansi did not utter a single word; he just gave me a surprising look.

Perhaps I turned down the Ambassador's invitation because I had felt he was overly hospitable.

29

During that trip, I came to realise that Mansi had some diplomatic talents that I had not noticed before. But these, like all his other talents, were chaotic and perhaps needed someone, such as me, to harness and steer them on the right course – only then would they turn into a truly creative power. Perhaps he had decided from the very beginning that he had a role to play in the mission that the State of Qatar had entrusted to me. I resigned myself to taking advantage of his company so I would take him along to my informal meetings. In a sense I had no choice, for both Dorga and his car were exclusively at Mansi's disposal.

So, I went alone to meetings with state officials while Mansi joined me when I had meetings with journalists, TV and broadcasting, as well as with senior executives of the media corporation that was founded by Nehru after Independence, like the institution that the Qataris had been contemplating.

We found out most of the media, particularly the English-language, were largely antagonistic to Mrs Gandhi, the

Prime Minister. As their titles suggested – the *Statesman*, *Times of India* – they followed the model of British newspapers.

We met with the chief editors of these two newspapers who showed deep enmity, almost personal hatred, towards Mrs Gandhi. That antagonism, I can say, spilled over to her foreign policy, particularly her support of Arab causes. Mansi fared well in these meetings, and his aggressiveness proved particularly useful in such circumstances.

We acted very much like two football players, working in perfect harmony. I would come up with an idea and he would pick it up and develop it, and I would bring it on course when I felt he had gone too far. Sometimes we would deliberately express divergent viewpoints so our audience would not think we were voicing the same clichés and propaganda. Being aware that the people we were going to meet had a blurred – to say the least – view of the Arab world, we were particularly keen to leave an impression of enlightened, civilised people. And since the people in our audience were largely intellectuals, we strived to make them feel that we were at least peers – I say 'at least' because Mansi was trying to make them believe that they were way inferior to him. In fact, that was not a particularly difficult endeavour, given my vested interest in India. Mansi, as usual, was very smart at using the scarce knowledge that he had in scoring higher than I could have hoped to achieve despite my wide knowledge of the country.

I was equally surprised to notice in Mansi, during that period, a zeal towards Islam that I had never noticed before.

You might ask: why had he embraced Islam in the first

place? I have no definite answer. What I do know is that he embraced Islam as smoothly as anyone would move from their home to the house next door. It was not driven by any business interest or other earthly desire. He used to say he had read the holy Qur'an with Muslim boys in the village of Mallawi in Upper Egypt, and he memorised some verses. That was not unusual, for the Copts of the Nile Valley had blood relations with Muslims. I do remember that Coptic boys used to recite the Qur'an with us at school and attend religion classes. I remember a Coptic classmate who used to recite the Qur'an in a lovely voice.

In the city of Omdurman, there is a district known as al-Masalma inhabited by Copts who had migrated from Egypt. Some of those converted to Islam, so you would find Muslims and *Nasaraa* in the same family. The same applies to Syria and Iraq too. In Lebanon, each one of these warring factions included both *Nasaraa* and Muslims. I am deliberately using the word *Nasaraa* because it is the word that has been used by Muslims and Arabs throughout history, meaning Nazarenes, that is, followers of Jesus, and is free from any hostile connotations. In fact, just the opposite – it is replete with meanings of mercy and good will. The word 'Christian' was fairly new.

We know that Arab *Nasaraa* supported Arab Muslims in the battles of Yarmouk and Qadisiyah. During the latter battle, the injured Muslim leader said to a *Nasrani* Arab: "It's true you do not belong to our creed, but you are our brother. So hold the flag on my behalf."

Thus, religious tolerance was an inherent feature of our

land and people. So what is the point of these wars in the name of religion and all this enmity, hatred, and feuds?

How long these disputes of yours are meant to last?
What's the point?
For whose sake are you plotting and intriguing?
Showing sheer enmity and hate?[13]

It is as if poets are destined to perpetually ask these questions through the course of history without any response — as if their questions always fall on deaf ears.

Mansi embraced Islam in Washington before the Imam of the mosque there. No sooner had he done so than he became a preacher, as though he had been Muslim from birth. He established a broadcasting service to propagate Islam and he lectured about Islam across America. He claimed that he had helped scores of people to embrace Islam. "How many did you?" he challenged me.

I might have softened the hearts of some, or helped clear up some misconceptions about Islam. But when it comes to whether I had actually helped anyone to embrace Islam, the answer is definitely no.

---

13 From a poem by Ahmed Shawqi

30

Dorga, Mansi's friend, came back carrying the tickets and the booking. Although the Qatari Embassy had instructed him to facilitate my mission and arrange my meetings, he put himself entirely at the service of Mansi and ignored me completely. Mansi was busy shopping; particularly in tailors' shops that could make you a full suit in one day. He found excellent quality textiles at cheap prices. Here also he found some old friends. I had always wondered how he could find friends wherever he went. As for me, I had work that had to be done. However, I had no option but to submit to this weird arrangement. I would meet Dorga coming up or down the stairs, or running around after 'Dr Ahmed'. Sometimes, I would stop him and try my best to tease him: "Where were you, Dorga? Weren't you supposed to take me to the TV station?"

But he would answer in his typical Indian cold tone that would infuriate anyone: "Sorry, Mr Salih, but Dr Ahmed had an important meeting."

It was obvious that Mansi had led him to understand that

it was he who was the principal envoy of the Qatari Government, and that I was no more than a member of his entourage.

Mansi would say, playfully: "Listen. Today you can take Dorga and the car. I don't need them. But on one condition – that I come with you."

I had no option but to let him accompany me, even to some of my formal meetings. To Dorga, that was further proof that Dr Ahmed was the principal envoy who deserved his service, while I was merely a companion.

But Dorga had gone then too far. I had asked him to book me on the plane to Sydney through Bangkok. Mansi had wanted to go through Bombay. I said to him: "At least we have seen one city in India. That should be enough. Let us see a new city in another country. Besides, Bangkok is on our route, while Bombay is further to the west."

He looked convinced, and that was why I was surprised when Dorga made the booking through Bombay.

"Didn't I tell you to make the booking through Bangkok?"

"Yes; but Dr Ahmed instructed me to make it to Bombay."

'Dr Ahmed' came back to the hotel in jubilant mood. I always wondered how he was able to find a reason for joy in each step. Is this life so replete with pleasures? Did he own a 'built-in' joy factory?

"Listen. I am going to Bangkok as I had originally planned. If you want to come with me to Bangkok you are welcome, otherwise, good bye."

"Don't be a fool. Forget about Bangkok. It's rubbish. I have to go to Bombay. I have an important business meeting there."

My God! I thought that his joining me on this trip was a coincidence; but then how had he found time to arrange an 'important meeting' in Bombay?

"I am not playing games, my friend. This is how business should be conducted: swiftly. You think money comes easily, effortlessly? You think bluffing can work in every situation?"

I could not help but laugh. He added: "Of course, some bluffing can help but you need to make some effort."

I said to myself: "Let him go to Bombay, and hopefully on to another destination far away so that I can have some time alone. After a week of the chaos and anarchy that sur-rounded Mansi, I longed to have time to myself. Now I can be myself, take residence wherever I want, wander in the streets of foreign cities, leisurely familiarise myself with new things, contemplate the scenes and store some into memory. I have my books and papers. And I have my treasure of deeply buried memories that can pop up unexpectedly, stirred by a sudden blow of wind, a flash of light, someone's voice, the sun rising or setting on an unfamiliar horizon. And I have my all-time companion: al-Mutanabbi the Great, the pioneer of horizons, and the victim of crossroads:

Although we know best, yet, in Najd we asked:
Is our path long, or would it be longer made?
Much asking is prompted by my longing,
While your responses are mostly flimsy promises.

*O let me feast my eyes on the beauty of your face while it
    lasts.*
For facial beauty is transitory and someday will be gone.
And let us enjoy intimate closeness while we yet live.
For life is short and our sojourn here is brief.

Look at these eloquent verses: That is how poetry should be. It is not "Is our path short or long? – For a road might seem much longer than what it actually is. This stanza is then followed by an eloquent verse that sums up what would take other poets a lengthy poem to express:

*No place on earth, away from your abode, is tempting
    enough to keep us,*
*All places wish if they could themselves get closer to your
    quarters.*

31

"Listen," the senior official at the Australian Department of Foreign Affairs said. "Selling wheat, butter and meat to the Arabs doesn't necessarily mean we have to back their political positions. Didn't you know that Australia is known as 'the lucky land'? We have everything – oil, agriculture and industry. Our country is spacious, an entire continent. It has bountiful riches. What else would we need the Arabs for?"

His remark bothered me though I liked his candidness and I had spent an hour or so debating with him. I noticed that he offered me no coffee or tea although I had come as early as 9 am.

"Don't you offer drinks to your guests? I guess it's coffee time, isn't it? Back in our country we offer coffee and tea to our guests."

Pressing the bell, he said: "Ah, sorry. Personally, I do not take these stimulants; they are not good for the health. And this administration has put an austerity policy in place. They say our economy is not faring well."

I was happy to lead him into that contradiction: a country replete with riches is in financial crisis and imposing austerity measures! I gave him exactly the same smile that the 'Master' [al-Mutanabbi] had recommended:

> *Since people's love has become tainted with hypocrisy,*
> *I have chosen to similarly deal with them:*
> *They greet me with a broad smile,*
> *I, likewise, smile broadly back at them.*

I was alone in Canberra, that beautiful city, with its spacious courtyards and lawn-covered parks, which had been designed to serve as Australia's administrative capital. Mansi and I had parted at Sydney Airport; he headed towards London while I flew to Canberra.

He could not make it with me to Tokyo. It was the first time that he appeared unable to achieve a goal. They told him that the only option he had was to go via Moscow or go back to London and then on to Tokyo. He almost convinced me that we should go together via Moscow. That was a world I knew nothing about except what I had read in books and newspapers. I wish I had gone – the Russians owed me royalties on the translations of my books that we could prosper on – as they would not hesitate to devour the property of orphans!

Yes, I wish we had gone. We know a lot about the West – England, France, Italy, Germany, and the USA. To us, that is 'the world' and we work hard to learn its languages and history, and we keep coming and going. We adore it but do not seem to get in return anything comparable with that love.

If what brings us together is our common love for you,
I wish we would meritoriously share your bounties,
Each according to the love he harbours for you.[14]

Yes, we love it and we eschew it. As for the Soviet Union, India, Japan and Latin America, they do not weigh much on our scales. Nor do our brothers and partners who helped us build our civilisation; Nor do the Africans, our neighbours and blood relatives.

I wish we could go. But I had a lot of work to do.

Had I exerted the slightest effort, I could have convinced Mansi to change his route and join me in Tokyo. But after ten days in his company I felt I had had enough of him and longed for my own company.

So I did my best to discourage him and urged him to go to Paris instead.

"Good idea. It has been a while since I last saw Barbara Bray. The weather in Paris should be great these days. But unfortunately we will miss you."

"Hopefully I will join you after coming back from Tokyo."

"This is the first time I encounter such a problem. They claim I had overrun my mileage allocation as a tourist company – Rubbish! I said to them: 'You fools! Isn't Tokyo nearer to here than from London? But what can we do? Complicated rules and stupid people."

---

14 Lines of al-Mutanabbi

"Don't feel sad. You have been to Tokyo before, haven't you?"

"More than ten times. I know every inch of Japan. Didn't you know that I know the Japanese language?"

"Come on! Stop it!"

"You don't believe me? Did you forget that I have a language school in Washington – modern facilities, audiovisuals and all that stuff? And I translated one of Mishima's stories into English. Of course, you haven't heard of Mishima!"

"Of course I have. But to claim that you have translated a story from Japanese to English is too far-fetched. Where did you publish it?

He gave out a laugh that suggested that his claim could be true and could be false, but that I had to take it for granted. Then he said: "You are certainly going to need me in Japan. I would have been a great help to you in your mission."

"No doubt about that. What to do? I will try to do the mission all by myself. I will do what I can. But I'm going to miss your resourcefulness and genius."

"You are mocking me? I truly am a genius. Why can't you admit this simple fact?"

"Listen, son. You are truly one of a kind, peerless, '*NASEEJ WAHDIHI*'! One who will never be repeated! But genius? I am not sure!"

"First of all, you need to learn to speak proper Arabic. You present yourself as a writer and all this bluff when your Arabic grammar is shamefully poor. It's not '*WAHDIHI*' – it should be '*WAHADAHO*'."

"Why?"

"Because it is indeclinable."

"Come on! It's a governed noun."

"How ignorant you are! Have you forgotten that I have a BA in Arabic from London University?"

I laughed because I knew how he had obtained that degree. I had helped him with his Arabic language and Arab history lessons. He could hardly differentiate between 'Abdel Malik ibn Marwan – whom he erroneously called 'Abdel Malik Abu Marwan' – and 'Abu Gaafar al-Mansour' – whom he called 'Abu Gaafar ibn Mansour'. On the day he obtained his degree, we were sitting in a café on Kings Road in Chelsea and got into an argument about language.

"Listen," I said. "Remember, I was your teacher. Without my assistance you couldn't have obtained your degree."

His laughter in reply confirmed this story. And he then said: "Let this alone now. Be fair and admit it: Didn't I afford great help to you in your mission? Together didn't we carry out excellent diplomatic work?"

"I admit you have demonstrated significant diplomatic talent."

"How did you find our debate with Mr Cameroon? Did you see how we astounded the man – you from one side and I from the other?"

"It was OK."

"And the young Palestinian man at ABS (Australian Broadcasting Service)? Didn't you notice? The moment I saw him I realised that he was an Arab. It was he who introduced you to the Australian director, and it was thanks to him that they conducted an interview with you for a full hour on their prime programme."

'That's true. I can't deny it."

'But you sneaked off and went alone to the interview – because you were afraid that I was going to steal the show from you."

"Of course. You could have. I am not as fluent as you are, doctor? Do you really hold a PhD?"

"Of course I do! Didn't you know? I have THREE – not only one!"

"Like Zaki Mubarak[15], eh? Show some fear of God, man!"

"Leave this now. Be fair and admit it: Wouldn't you and I have made amazing roving ambassadors? Imagine if they appointed us as ambassadors to serve the Arab cause: wouldn't that have been more beneficial than all this nonsense?"

More than ten days in the throes of this clutter, I began to feel fed up with Mansi and yearn for loneliness. That was why I did not encourage him to go with me to Tokyo. However, as we sat in Sydney Airport – he heading to London and I to Canberra – a feeling of sadness had overwhelmed me. And when his plane took off, I wished I had given him a hug. Now, as I was facing this arrogant man at the Department of Foreign Affairs, I thought of Mansi and wished he had been with me. His flippancy could have been a great help in such a situation.

---

15 The prominent Egyptian scholar, "a man of letters and of poetry"

32

"Look, Tayeb," Mansi had suddenly said, as we were walking along the corridors of the Australian Broadcasting Service, "I bet you that young man is an Arab." Before I could say a word, Mansi ran to him: "Hi, brother. You are an Arab, right?" he said in Arabic.

We were just out of a business lunch with the Director General and senior executives of the Australian Broadcasting Service. Mansi was all smiles as he entered the meeting, all giggles as he came out. Perhaps he remembered his days at the BBC in London, racing in his bubble car between Caversham and Bush House to translate or act in return for a few pounds. All his resourcefulness could not help him get to the Director General, who was beyond reach. He had come a long way. Here also was a 'corporation', and here also was a 'director general'. Mansi entered all smiles; wearing a fur overcoat, a fine woollen suit, and Italian shoes of high quality leather. To those who did not know him, he looked like a completely different 'Mansi'. But I was aware that it was all superficial, very much like camouflage, like a costume an actor would put on while on stage.

May God rest his soul in peace, he was now acting as an ambassador standing in defence of the dignity and reputation of Arabs, a role he was neither commissioned nor paid to play yet he performed it in the best possible way. Perhaps he was right – had an important assignment been entrusted to him, he would have discharged it perfectly well. Yet he had never been called upon; all the roles he had played had been very much his own initiative, roles that he had imposed on himself to play. In fact, all the roles he had played were unsolicited.

When he talked at the luncheon, he sounded like a senior Arab official who could well be an advisor to a ruler or to a head of state – he deliberately left it vague, and as usual, he frequently mixed serious talk with jesting, taking advantage of his eloquent English, quick-wittedness, and resourcefulness.

Whenever he felt he was in trouble, he would look at me in a way that would suggest I was his aide. That was perfectly okay with me because it provided me with the rare chance to take part in the conversation and observe Mansi at the same time: as if I was both an actor and a spectator at the same time.

Our conversation covered diverse topics. Our hosts were enlightened gentlemen who would use reason and argument to present and defend their opinions. Mansi did not sound rude when he said, as if in jest: "It's quite obvious to us that your media is nothing more than an echo of the Western media, with the same prejudice against us, the same disdain and defaming – all boring stuff that we have got used to."

He laughed when he uttered the word "defaming" and it occurred to me that he deliberately used that particular word instead of the more commonly used expression "image tarnishing". We had arrived in Australia only four days before, and it was Mansi's first visit to this part of the world of which he hardly had any knowledge. It seemed part of his nature to blurt out anything that would come to his mind; to throw out his arrow and be little bothered if it hit or missed the target.

Although they were clearly taken aback, the smart, experienced gentlemen quickly tried to conceal their feelings in different ways. Some smiled. Some laughed.

"Wait a minute, Dr Michael," said the Director General. "That's unfair. You know that the ABS is an autonomous body. Even the Government has no control over it. It is an entirely neutral organisation. We cover world affairs in all objectivity. We have absolutely no reason to be prejudiced against the Arabs or to defame them, as you put it."

As if the man wanted to take refuge with me away from Mansi, he said: "Do you too hold this opinion, Mr Salih?"

It was clear beyond doubt that Mansi's statement, particularly that part about defaming, had hit a sensitive nerve. The Australians too had a feeling that the world cared little for them, did not give them the recognition they deserved, and was prejudiced against them in most cases. There is hardly any nation that has no cause for embarrassment or shame in her history: The Japanese treatment of prisoners during Second Word War; the Germans' atrocities against the Jews and others; the Americans dropping nuclear bombs on Hiroshima and Nagasaki; the French massacres in Algeria, the Britons' invention of detention camps, and their heinous acts in Palestine and Africa. The Russians, the Chinese, the Spanish, the Portuguese – you name it. Only a few nations can claim that they have no act that they feel sorry for. So why should all the blame fall exclusively on the Arabs? And how come it turned out as if they were the perpetrators of all the crimes in history? These are questions that Arabs ought to find answers for before blaming others.

I said: "I am not exactly sure what programmes you are broadcasting – we haven't been here long enough. Yet the little I have seen, particularly news bulletin, does suggest to me that Dr Michael was not very wrong. As for your papers, it's clear that their coverage of Arab world events is driven by misinformation or ill-intentions."

As if he was reading my thoughts, Mansi picked up the argument I was about to make. "Yes. Your papers in particular," he said. "Rarely would one open a paper without coming across a mention of that stupid film, that one full of lies whose sole objective is to insult the Arabs."

That was the focus of media in Europe, the USA and even here in Australia at the time, just as the "Salman Rushdie affair" is these days. Every now and then, they come up with something new that is designed to cause controversy and confusion.

"In all cases," one official commented, "you have got only yourselves to blame. There is no conspiracy against the

Arabs, as you think. It is all about the lack of the required information at the right time. You are not helping us. You are not helping anyone get access to information. More than that, you often create obstacles. Your media has not yet realised that the world has become connected together and that it's now the information age."

The Director General, who was the most cheerful amongst them, said: "And remember – Arabs do commit indecent acts sometimes. So what would you expect us to do? Cover them up? Keep them in the dark, as is your usual practice?"

Typical of Mansi, he would not let this go without comment.

"And is what you do always decent?" he fired back, his face radiating with a malicious laugh.

At this point, the man raised his hand submissively, and we moved away from the table, each one of us either smiling or laughing. Mansi was the happiest amongst us; for it was he who carried the Arab flag high in that remote corner of the globe. He masterfully played a role that no one had commissioned or paid him to do – a role for which he did not hear a single word of thanks after playing it. His only gain was personal passion.

They were truly nice gentlemen. We were hoping that we left them with some positive ideas that might bear fruit some day, or as Mansi frequently loved to say: "Throw your good deeds on the surface of the water: they are destined to bear fruit later if not sooner."

Then as we were walking along the hallway, we came

across that young man. Mansi stopped him. "Excuse me, brother. You are an Arab, aren't you?" he asked him.

Yes, he was an Arab, a Palestinian immigrant, an employee of ABS. His name, if I remember well, was Ibrahim al-Khouri.

33

In the evening of that same day, the young Palestinian visited us at the hotel. As it turned out, Mansi had done us a favour by calling out to him. For he became our guide, opening doors for us, clearing obstacles and leading us through this alien land, and introducing us to the Arab community in Sydney. Of course, Mansi did not forget to add that to the long list of favours he had done me. From that moment on, he would remind me time and again, whenever he had the chance, that he was so smart and sharp to immediately identify that young man as an Arab as we walked along the ABS corridors following our luncheon with the Director General.

"Tell them, Tayeb ... Wasn't that what happened? I identified him instantly while you were walking along absentmindedly. And, honestly, wasn't it I who made your mission a success? You couldn't have achieved anything without me. Tell them, please, about my performance at the luncheon with the Director General – the man was stunned!"

We were in Riyadh. Now, each time I visit Riyadh, I think of Mansi the moment I step into the airport. On my first visit there, at the invitation of Sheikh Abdulaziz al-Tuwaijri, I found Mansi seated in a big car waiting for me, right by the plane's boarding steps. He laughed upon seeing me, in a way that suggested to me that this welcoming gesture was less a show of warm hospitality than a demonstration of his own influence and leverage. The Sheikh had assigned him to arrange my stay and travel, which he did perfectly well – he loved such assignments.

He had accompanied me on my first Umrah – the first Umrah has a special taste that you hardly get in subsequent ones. Now whenever I visited those shrines I would seem to see an image of him racing between Mount Safa and Mount Marwa, exhaustedly pulling his heavy body, hanging his arms to the Kaaba, or sound asleep on the floor, between the sunset and evening prayers, little bothered by the waves of worshippers.

That visit was a blessing to Mansi in many respects. He booked a hotel suite near mine, for him and his wife, and charged the cost to my visit's account. That became a constant practice in my subsequent visits, and in the rare cases when he chose not to take advantage of the free hotel stay, he would still deliver his clothes for laundry and dry cleaning.

It was also in Riyadh that he once joined me in prayers. I had not been fully convinced that he had converted to Islam until that day when I stood up to perform Maghrib (sunset) prayers. He simply approached and lined himself beside me. My goodness! We were brothers in humanity, now we had become brothers in faith!

That occasion was the last time we met in Riyadh. He had found a job in a company. He did not really need a job; it was only that he always wanted to preoccupy himself with something. He enjoyed having an office, a doorman, a secretary, and a telephone, ideally at someone's expense, although he could have easily provided for these items from his own resources.

I would say to him: "Shouldn't you just go back to England to live on your estate now? Do you really need a job and salary? Go and enjoy your wealth before you die and leave it to your heirs!"

"Die? What are you talking about? There is still a long way to go before I get to that station. Many things still remain to be done."

Death was not on his agenda. He was too preoccupied with life to remember death.

"Do you think I have much to do here?" he said between his fits of laughter. "I need an hour maximum to finish my work; then I devote the entire time that is left to running my own business. Where else would I find these facilities – telex, fax, phones, typists – all free of charge?"

"And what exactly is your role?"

"Compiling reports for the manager."

"Financial reports?"

"No. That is handled by some other people. I am a personal advisor to the general manager for a wide range of areas: media, PR, international communication, and the like.

And, mind you, I am the number two man in the company, right after the GM. Every morning I write a report for the GM — a roundup of foreign press news and analysis, and that trivial stuff. I bet you, even at the Foreign Office they can't do analyses as good as mine."

"But what is the use of these for the GM of a commercial company?"

"Of course they are immensely valuable. Do you still think of business as selling and buying, exports and imports? We are not running a grocery in Omdurman, for God's sake. This is proper business: high-level connections, devious games, etc. Besides, the GM is a highly educated chap, he holds an MBA from the States. Unfortunately, he is out of town or I would have introduced you to him ... a cute guy. You would have loved him. His father is a cousin of ... His mother is ... He is married to the daughter of ..."

"Leave this now and tell me in all honesty, is the company benefitting from you in any way?"

"Of course it is! The GM would not let go of me. But, between you and me, I am intending to leave. As you said, what would I need the money for?"

Mansi held numerous jobs during his short stay in Riyadh. He was too moody to stick to one for a good while — and Sheikh Abdulaziz al-Tuwaijri and his son, Abdul Mohsin, were always there to help him out and find him another job whenever he walked out of one.

I had no alternative but to heed his persistent requests and visit him at his office. He wanted me to see how important and influential he was, although I hardly needed proof. He was accorded a warm welcome by a parade of office boys, doormen and labourers. He joked with them and it was obvious that they had a deep affection for him. That was typical of him: down to earth, always on close terms with the poor and modest. They kept coming to his office, one after the other, seeking his help with a cocktail of problems – residence permit, a pay problem, medical care for a sick wife. He was cheerful, inflated with a feeling of pride and a strong urge to help those helpless people.

He drew my attention to the office furniture, the carpet, the curtains, the table, the chairs, the phone sets, the safes, the indoor plants, the flowers – introducing them to me one after the other in the same way as he would introduce humans.

"Look, Tayeb. Look at this carpet. This is no regular stuff, by the way. It's Persian – a rare one!"

"Really? How much is it worth?"

"Oooh! A fortune. Surely more than your pay for a full year!"

"Wonderful! Did you pay for it from your own pocket?"

"Why should I? Do you think I am an idiot, as Cairo residents say of *saeedis*? Of course, I got it at the company's expense. By the way, I am the only one who has an office like this. The GM thinks very highly of me. He wouldn't let go of me . . ."

I looked at the telephones, each in a different colour. Why would one need many phones when he can hear with only one ear? Why would one need more than one car? But

Mansi was not one, he was many sharing one body.

The moment I entered his house in the evening, I saw cars lined up like horses in a stable. He insisted on taking me on a tour, exactly as one would tour a museum. Here was the pool: he had a strong passion for swimming – he swam like a hippopotamus. Then the garages and a cocktail of cars of different makes; he later moved many of those to his estate in Southampton. The gardens, the trees, the rare plants, the drivers' and workers' quarters, and the Filipino housemaids' quarters.

"This is massive!"

"Did you like it? Mind you, all this is free of charge, apart from the salary."

Life was definitely joking with him; apparently, life treats everyone the way they are.

That was the last time we met in Saudi Arabia. I never saw him as happy as he was that night, laughing and laughing, carrying his son, Ahmed, who was a perfect copy of him, particularly when he laughed.

We were accorded a warm hospitality that night and he found a big audience and a "favourable wind", so he was his usual uninhibited self, while I acted as his support, prodding him and giving him leads.

"Tell them, Tayeb, what we did in Australia . . . we surely did amazing things! Admit it, wasn't it I who told you that chap was an Arab but you didn't want us to stop?

That Palestinian chap had come to us there in the evening and from that moment on he became our guide in Sydney. Among the many favours he accorded us was to introduce

us to a Lebanese gentleman, who was one of those rare per-
sonalities that on meeting them you feel life has bestowed
upon you unforgettable good fortune.

34

News about our presence in Sydney spread fast and Mansi spared no effort to lend grandeur to our visit. The Arab community was in a pathetic state of disarray and discord; perhaps they thought we were mediators. That was not true as no one had solicited us to undertake such a mission. It was Mansi who volunteered to play the role of conciliator. Arabs show profound affection for their compatriots while away from their homeland but do not seem to stand each other while at home. We were strangers, so they welcomed us as a native dweller would welcome a strange guest, although in fact they were more alienated than us.

We received scores of visitors. Mansi became more cheerful with each new visit. He was at his best. Here again, he was the leading actor on a huge stage, undertaking a highly important role: a conciliator and a good office messenger. Our Palestinian friend was by our side most of the time, supporting and encouraging, showing us around and introducing us to people. The Palestinians, who had been dealt particularly cruel blows of fate, were naturally more eager than anyone else to see Arabs stand as a united faction, although they themselves were not immune to discord within their own ranks.

We were visited by George Samaan and his brother, Michel, Lebanese publishers of an Arabic newspaper with a circulation of 20 to 30 thousand copies. It was a highly respected paper addressing issues of interest to the Arab community at large, doing its best to steer away from paths of discord. They complained to me about meagre resources and lack of support in their admirable effort to keep members of the Arabic community in Australia together and link them to the Arab motherland. I tried my best, upon my return, to help them and I believe they did receive some aid from the Gulf Cooperation Council.

We were visited by people of all walks of life, government employees, business persons, media professionals. For our part, we took the initiative of visiting the imam of the mosque and the archbishop of the Maronite Community in Australia.

I remember that latter gentleman very well: down to earth, solemn, serene, kind-hearted; he was a personification of the traits of ancient Christian clergymen as described in the Holy Qur'an. He was well versed in Islamic jurisprudence, Hadith, history, and Arab culture and he held a PhD in Islamic Jurisprudence from the Sorbonne. He managed to keep himself away from inter-Arab feuds and successfully resisted all pressure and temptations to side with any of Lebanon's warring factions.

The Arab community at the time was around 300,000;

most of them lived in the two major cities, Sydney and Melbourne. The Lebanese were the largest group. Their emigration to Australia had begun in the past century, driven by successive wars and famines, as is the case today. While some intermingled with fellow immigrant communities, others remained faithful to their Lebanese identity. All of them invariably harboured a deep nostalgia for their war-scarred home country. Life in exile did little to weaken that attachment and they continued to eat *kibbeh, tabbouleh* and *shawarma*, and listen to the charming songs of Wadih El Safi, Sabah and Fairouz.

The second largest Arab community, after the Lebanese, was the Egyptian. Compared to the former, they were fairly recent immigrants who had not yet severed ties with Egypt. They still went home whenever they could, and would give you the impression that, given the option, they would prefer to return home; in fact, some would eventually make it.

The Palestinians ranked third. They had scattered to every corner of the globe. They migrated in successive waves; with each calamity hitting their homeland, they fled in search of a safe haven elsewhere. You see them wherever you go, in Canada, the US, and across Europe. There is something in their faces that distinguishes them from other Arab immigrants: they look more resolved, more grieved, with an evident streak of bitterness. They are harbouring a dream that sometimes seems attainable and at other instances proves to be beyond reach.

We also found, albeit in smaller numbers, Yemenis, Syrians, Somalis, Moroccans and some Sudanese Copts. The number of Sudanese must have increased by now, all of them were highly experienced and skilled professionals, many held high qualifications in medicine, engineering, agriculture and other disciplines; some took up lecturer positions at universities. Australia is particularly selective in admitting expatriates.

The Arab world's calamities and feuds continued to haunt those immigrants even in exile, as if what was going on back at home was not bad enough. If they were left alone, they could have settled more comfortably in this distant land. Here they were all strangers, struggling with life. They were all the same in the eyes of the Australians, and they could have achieved things that the Arab world at large would be proud of.

What we found, alas, was an Arab world in microcosm: the same divisions, the same feuds, the same trivialities. A world in turmoil, echoing the follies and hostilities of the homeland, if I may call it so. They seemed like animals that have lost the survival instinct, or passengers at each other's throats while their ship wrestled with a rough sea.

Fortunately, however, the imam of the Muslims and the archbishop of the Maronites remained on good terms. They were friends, exchanging visits and joining hands for noble causes. So we would meet people at the imam's house on one occasion and at the archbishop's on another.

They say things have changed now in the Arab world and, by definition, in Australia. I hope so, but we will believe this only when the war has come to an end in Lebanon and Sudan, as well as in all Muslim and Arab countries. When that happens, migrating birds will return to their nests and nights will be thrilling and amusing again, and even that cherished dream of returning to the Palestinian homeland will not be far beyond reach any more.

Tayeb Salih

Tayeb Salih (1929–2009) is renowned as one of the 20th century's greatest authors, particularly for his novel *Season of Migration to the North*, which was first published in Arabic in 1966 and in English translation by his friend Denys Johnson-Davies in 1969. In 2001 the Arab Literary Academy declared *Season of Migration to the North* to be 'the most important Arabic novel of the 20th century' and it remains a pivotal point in post-colonial narrative. It is translated into more than 20 languages, and has never been out of print in English, in a number of different editions. Other fiction works by Tayeb Salih translated into English by Denys Johnson-Davies include *The Doum Tree of Wad Hamid* (1960, English 1962, *Encounter* magazine), *The Wedding of Zein* (1962, English 1968), the short story *A Handful of Dates* (1964, English 1968), and *Bandarshah* (Arabic 1971 and 1976, English 1996), mostly set around Sudanese village life. Tayeb Salih was born in Karmakol, near al-Dabbah in northern Sudan. He graduated from the University of Khartoum, and then left Sudan to study at the University of London, but soon began working at the BBC's Arabic Service. For 10 years he wrote a weekly column for the London-based *Al-Majalla* magazine. He later worked as director-general of the Ministry of Information in Doha, Qatar, and spent 10 years with UNESCO, becoming its representative in the Gulf.

Adil Babikir

Adil Babikir is a Sudanese translator and writer based in the UAE. His published translations include *Modern Sudanese Poetry: an Anthology* (University of Nebraska Press, 2019); *The Jungo: Stakes of the Earth*, a novel by Abdelaziz Baraka Sakin (Africa World Press, USA, 2015); *Literary Sudans: an Anthology of Literature from Sudan and South Sudan,* edited by Bhakti Shringarpure, (Red Sea Press, USA, 2016); *Summer Maze*, a collection of short stories by Leila Aboulela, translated to Arabic (Dar al-Musawwarat, Khartoum, 2017). Babikir is a contributing editor of *Banipal* Magazine. Some of his translations appeared in *Banipal, The Guardian, Al-Doha* magazine, and *Jalada Africa*. His forthcoming works include two books by the late Abdul Khaliq Mahjub, one by Ustaz Mahmoud Mohammed Taha, a collection of Sudanese short novels and a book on the legendary Bedouin poet al-Hardallo.

ACKNOWLEDGEMENTS

The translator thanks Dr Mahmoud Abbas Masoud for translating some of the poetry citations used in the book, and Dina Omer Osman for her helpful edits of the text.

The translation of the lines of poetry by Zuhayr Ibn Abu Sulma is by A J Arberry, and can be found in *The Seven Odes*, London: George Allen & Unwin Ltd, 1957.

OTHER TITLES FROM BANIPAL BOOKS

Goat Mountain by Habib Selmi
ISBN: 978-1-913043-04-9 • Paperback • 92pp • 2020
Translated from the Arabic by Charis Olszok. The author's debut
novel, from 1988, now in English translation. The journey to
Goat Mountain, a forlorn, dusty, desert Tunisian village, begins in
a dilapidated old bus. "I enjoyed this book. I liked its gloomy
atmosphere, its strangeness and sense of unfamiliarity. Eerie,
funereal, and outstanding!" – Jabra Ibrahim Jabra

The Mariner by Taleb Alrefai
ISBN: 978-1-913043-08-7 • Paperback • 160pp • 2020
Translated from the Arabic by Russell Harris. A fictional re-
telling of the final treacherous journey at sea of famous Kuwaiti
dhow shipmaster Captain Al-Najdi, with flashbacks to the
awesome pull of the sea on Al-Najdi since childhood, his years
pearl fishing and the industry's demise, and his voyages around the
Arabian Peninsula with Australian sailor Alan Villiers.

A Boat to Lesbos, and other poems by Nouri Al-Jarrah
ISBN: 978-0-9956369-4-1 • Paperback • 120pp • 2018
Translated from the Arabic by Camilo Gómez-Rivas and Allison
Blecker and illustrated with paintings by Reem Yassouf. The first
English-language collection for this major Syrian poet, whose
compelling epic poem bears passionate witness to Syrian families
fleeing to Lesbos through the eye of history, of Sappho and the
travels of Odysseus.

An Iraqi In Paris by Samuel Shimon
ISBN: 978-0-9574424-8-1 • Paperback • 282pp • 2016
Translated from the Arabic by Christina Philips and Piers
Amodia with the author. Long-listed for the 2007 IMPAC Prize.
Called a gem of autobiographical writing, a manifesto of
tolerance, a cinematographic odyssey. "This combination of a
realist style with content more akin to the adventures of Sindbad
helps to make *An Iraqi in Paris* a modern Arab fable, sustaining
the moral such a fable requires: follow your dreams and you will
succeed" – Hanna Ziadeh, *Al-Ahram Weekly*

Heavenly Life: Selected Poems by Ramsey Nasr
ISBN: 978-0-9549666-9-0 • Paperback • 180pp • 2010
First English-language collection for Ramsey Nasr, Poet Laureate
of the Netherlands, 2009 & 2010. Translated from the Dutch by
David Colmer, with an Introduction by Victor Schiferli and a
Foreword by Ruth Padel. The title poem was written to
commemorate the 150th anniversary of Gustav Mahler's birth
and is based on his Fourth Symphony, the four sections of the
poem echoing the structure, tone and length of its movements. It
is named after "Das himmlische Leben", the song that forms the
symphony's finale.

Knife Sharpener: Selected Poems by Sargon Boulus.
ISBN: 978-0-9549666-7-6 • Paperback • 154pp • 2009
The first English-language collection for this influential and
innovative Iraqi poet, who dedicated himself to reading, writing
and translating into Arabic contemporary poetry. Foreword by
Adonis. Translated from the Arabic by the author with an essay
"Poetry and Memory". Also tributes by fellow poets and authors
following the author's passing while the book was in production
and an Afterword by the publisher.

Shepherd of Solitude: Selected Poems by Amjad Nasser.
ISBN: 978-0-9549666-8-3 • Paperback • 186pp • 2009
The first English-language collection for this major modern
poet, who lived most of his life outside his home country of
Jordan. Translated from the Arabic and introduced by the
foremost translator of contemporary Arabic poetry into English,
Khaled Mattawa, with the poems selected by poet and translator
from the poet's Arabic volumes from the years 1979 to 2004.

**Mordechai's Moustache and his Wife's Cats, and other
stories** by Mahmoud Shukair.
ISBN: 978-0-9549666-3-8 • Paperback • 124 pages • 2007
Translations from the Arabic by Issa J Boullata, Elizabeth
Whitehouse, Elizabeth Winslow and Christina Phillips. This first
major publication in an English translation of one of the most
original of Palestinian storytellers enthralls, surprises and even
shocks. "Shukair's gift for absurdist satire is never more telling
than in the hilarious title story" – Judith Kazantsis

A Retired Gentleman, and other stories by Issa J Boullata
ISBN: 978-0-9549666-6-9 • Paperback • 120 pages • 2007
The Jerusalem-born author, scholar, critic, and translator creates a
rich medley of tales by emigrants to Canada and the US from
Palestine, Lebanon, Egypt and Syria. George, Kamal, Mayy,
Abdullah, Nadia, William all have to begin their lives again, learn
how to deal with their memories, with their pasts . . .

The Myrtle Tree by Jad El Hage.
ISBN: 978-0-9549666-4-5 • Paperback • 288 pages • 2007
"This remarkable novel, set in a Lebanese mountain village,
conveys with razor-sharp accuracy the sights, sounds, tastes and
tragic dilemmas of Lebanon's fratricidal civil war. A must read" –
Patrick Seale

Unbuttoning the Violin
Poems & short stories from Banipal Live 2006
ISBN: 0-9549666-2-7 • Paperback • 128pp • 2006
Selected works by poets Joumana Haddad from Lebanon and
Abed Ismael from Syria, and fiction writers Mansoura Ez-Eldin
from Egypt and Ala Hlehel from Palestine. The 2006 Banipal
Live UK tour was a partnership of Banipal magazine with the
British Council and The Reading Agency.

Sardines and Oranges: Short Stories from North Africa
ISBN: 978-0-9549666-1-4 • Paperback • 222 pages • 2005
Introduced by Peter Clark. The 26 stories are by 21 authors:
Latifa Baqa, Ahmed Bouzfour, Rachida el-Charni, Mohamed
Choukri, Mohammed Dib, Tarek Eltayeb, Mansoura Ez-Eldin,
Gamal el-Ghitani, Said al-Kafrawi, Idriss el-Kouri, Ahmed el-
Madini, Ali Mosbah, Hassouna Mosbahi, Sabri Moussa,
Muhammad Mustagab, Hassan Nasr, Rabia Raihane, Tayeb Salih,
Habib Selmi, Izz al-Din Tazi and Mohammed Zefzaf.
Translations are from the Arabic except for Mohammed Dib's
story, which was from the French original.